Vegetable
Growing
for
Southern Gardens

Vegetable Growing for Southern Gardens

William D. Adams,
Harris County
Extension Horticulturist

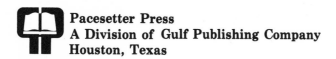

Pacesetter Press
A Division of Gulf Publishing Company
Houston, Texas

VEGETABLE GROWING FOR SOUTHERN GARDENS

Library of
Congress
Catalog Card
Number 75-18204
ISBN
0-88415-889-6

Illustrations by Terry J. Moore

**To my Grandmother
and her beautiful garden
and the many hours we spent
looking at seed catalogs**

Acknowledgments

This book could not have been completed without the support of my wife, Sandra. Holly and Josh wanted to help more. At the tender age of 3, Holly enjoys planting seeds, and Josh, 2, likes to pull weeds, onions and anything else that gets in his way.

This book is a partial answer to the question: "What will you do after you graduate with a degree in Horticulture?" It is also the product of having the privilege of working for the Texas Agricultural Extension Service.

I owe special thanks to my parents, who never required me to be anything other than what I wanted to be.

I was fortunate to acquire a second set of parents, Marge and Eldon, when I married Sandra. Also, Aunt Lois and Uncle Harold have been generous in many ways. We appreciate their love most of all.

This book would never have been completed without the concern of a friend, Bill Minar; the professional editorial work by B.J. Lowe; and the magnificent artwork and layout by Susan Corte, Terry Moore and David Price. There would have been no beginning without Clayton Umbach's interest and recognition of the need for regional garden books.

The technical assistance of Don Portie, Dr. Roland Roberts and Tom Longbrake in reading portions of the manuscript, and the wealth of valuable information supplied by other Agricultural Extension Service employees is sincerely appreciated.

Finally, Betsy Jones, who typed the manuscript evenings and on weekends is to be commended for making order out of chaos.

Preface

The South is famous for its gardens. It's not nearly so famous for its garden writers. Unfortunately, when the "green thumb urge" strikes, the southern gardener is often left with few books to turn to other than those written by northern authors. Perhaps these authors have more time to write "while the snow flies." During the same time the wise southern gardener is busy tilling, planting, and harvesting his garden. There's no reason why something can't be planted in or harvested from the southern garden every day of the year.

The information contained in northern garden books can often do you more harm than good, especially if you're a beginner. Gardeners in every region need their own publication; the United States is simply too large for one garden book to cover every subject everyplace, or even one subject everyplace.

Not since the days of the Victory Garden has there been so much enthusiasm for home vegetable gardening. Public enemy #1 is inflation, and planting a backyard vegetable garden is one of the best, and most enjoyable, ways to offset today's soaring food costs.

Even if you don't save money, or if your harvest is meager, you'll still have the satisfaction of having grown your own food and knowing what *fresh* produce really means. Besides, gardening is just plain fun.

Vegetable Growing for Southern Gardens was written in the South *for* southern gardeners. The latest information on soil preparation, soil amendments, raised beds, mini-gardens, and irrigation is presented and geared specifically for the South. Vegetables and herbs adapted to the South are discussed individually, along with specific details on their history, cultural and harvesting requirements, recommended varieties, and the diseases and pests which attack them. Much of the cultural information is also presented in convenient table form. Sample garden plans are included for both cool and warm season crops in mini, medium and large-garden sizes. These gardens schemes depict crops that actually grow together in southern gardens.

I think you'll find *Vegetable Growing for Southern Gardens* the best garden manual south of the Mason-Dixon line.

Bill Adams

Contents

Getting the Garden Started

Site Selection; Draw Your Plan; Planting Diagrams; Cool Season Garden; Warm Season Vegetables; Vegetables to Stagger Plant; Vegetables That Yield Over A Long Period of Time; Trellising.

What Makes a Good Soil?

Removing the Groundcover; Tilling; Loam; Clay and Sandy Soils; Organic Matter; Manure; Other Soil Amendments; Fertilizers; Composting; What's ph?; Instructions for Taking Soil Samples.

Planting, Thinning, Watering, Mulching

Average Frost Dates for Southern Cities; How To Be The First on Your Block with Vegetables; Grow Your Own Transplants; Materials You Will Need; Starting the Seedlings; Transplanting Procedures; Coldframes and Hotframes; Continuing Care of Seedlings; Watering; Drip Irrigation; Mulching; Black Plastic and Special Paper Mulches.

Controlling Those Pests

Natural Disease and Pest Controls; Chemical Pesticides; Insecticides; Fungicides; Keeping Varmints Out of The Garden; Insects and Pests.

What to Grow

Some Planting Hints for the Southern Gardener; Planting Chart; Cool Season Vegetables: Beets, Broccoli, Brussels Sprouts, Cabbage, Carrots, Cauliflower, Collards, Kohlrabi, Lettuce, Mustard Greens, Onions, English Peas, Irish Potatoes, Radishes, Spinach, Turnips; Other Cool Season Vegetables; Asparagus, A Perennial Vegetable; Swiss Chard, A Year-Round Vegetable; Warm Season Vegetables: Beans, Sweet Corn, Cucumber, Eggplant, Cantaloupe (Muskmelon), Okra, Southern Peas, Peppers, Sweet Potatoes, Pumpkin and Squash, Watermelon, Tomatoes, Caged Tomatoes, Fertilizer Cans; Other Warm Season Vegetables.

of special interest...

Getting the Garden Started

SITE SELECTION

Most gardeners have little choice about where to situate their gardens because of the limited size of today's lots. Finding a spot with fertile, deep, friable, well-drained soil may be impossible. Hopefully, you'll be able to locate the garden in full sun, away from competing trees and shrubs. Yet even this may be impossible. If lack of sun is a problem, you'll be restricted to growing leafy and root vegetables that tolerate partial shade, such as:

Beets	Lettuce
Brussels sprouts	Mustard
Cabbage	Parsley
Carrots	Radish
Collards	Spinach
Kale	Turnips
Endive	Climbing Spinach (Malabar)

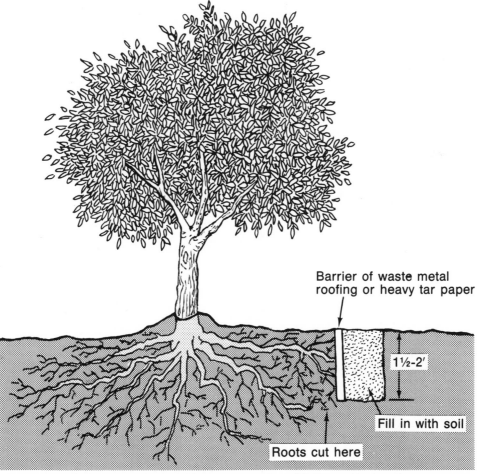

Barrier of waste metal roofing or heavy tar paper

1½-2'

Fill in with soil

Roots cut here

Invasive tree roots can be prevented from competing with the garden by digging a trench 1½ to 2 feet deep between the trees and the garden and cutting all the roots found crossing this area. To prevent regrowth into the garden put a barrier of metal roofing or heavy tar paper along one wall of the trench and refill it. This should eliminate root competition for several years.

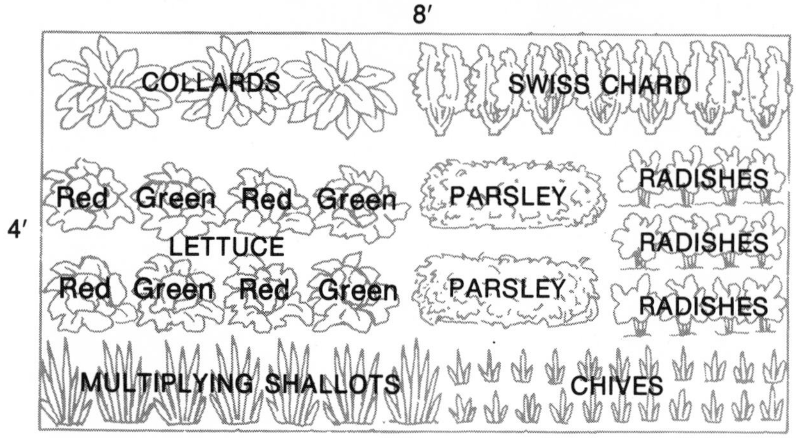

COLLARDS **SWISS CHARD**

Red Green Red Green **PARSLEY** **RADISHES**
LETTUCE **RADISHES**
Red Green Red Green **PARSLEY** **RADISHES**

MULTIPLYING SHALLOTS **CHIVES**

8'

4'

Garden layouts. Don't pay much attention to the garden plans and diagrams showing red ripe tomatoes, luscious green lettuce, cabbages, carrots, beets and other miscellaneous cold and warm season vegetables all in the same garden. In the South tomatoes may be planted at the same time your last crop of lettuce from the winter is fading out, but, unfortunately, our summers are not mild enough to allow harvesting most cold and warm season vegetables simultaneously.

(Left) Small, cool season garden, 4' x 8'.

(Below and on opposite page) Large, cool season garden, 50' x 100'.

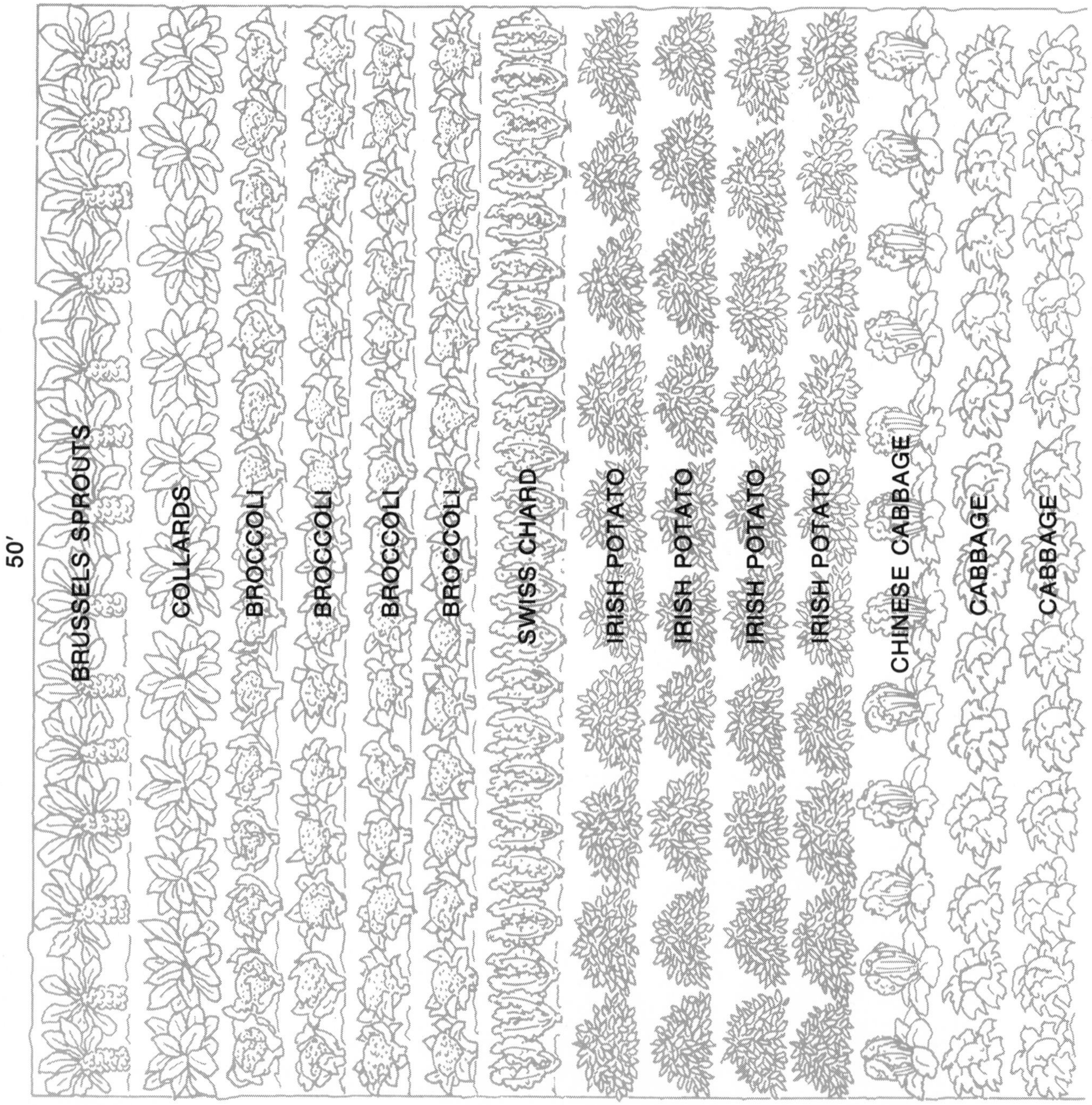

BRUSSELS SPROUTS COLLARDS BROCCOLI BROCCOLI BROCCOLI BROCCOLI SWISS CHARD IRISH POTATO IRISH POTATO IRISH POTATO IRISH POTATO CHINESE CABBAGE CABBAGE CABBAGE

50'

DRAW YOUR PLAN

When you've decided where to locate the garden, draw up a planting plan on graph paper. Remember, you'll need several plans—one for warm season vegetables, one for cool season vegetables, and perhaps several others with short season and companion crops shown.

Arrange rows in an east-west direction, with the tallest plants on the north side to prevent shading. Allow for pathways, particularly where you have spaced vegetables closely, and drive a few stakes at the end of rows to prevent water hoses from dragging across tender vegetation.

Planting Diagrams

Planting diagrams are at best a guide. Chances are your garden may never actually look like your diagram. As you begin to experiment with gardening you'll want to try companion planting: pumpkins in the corn, pole beans in the corn, or cucumbers with okra. Rapidly-maturing crops such as radishes or lettuce can be planted in and between rows of larger plants indicated in the garden diagram. You may even want to have a row of cut flowers in the garden.

(Text continued on page 7)

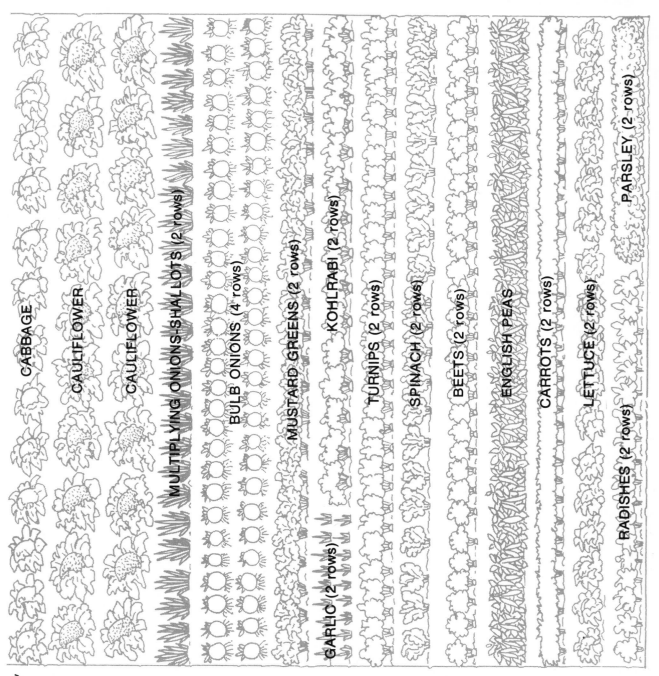

100'

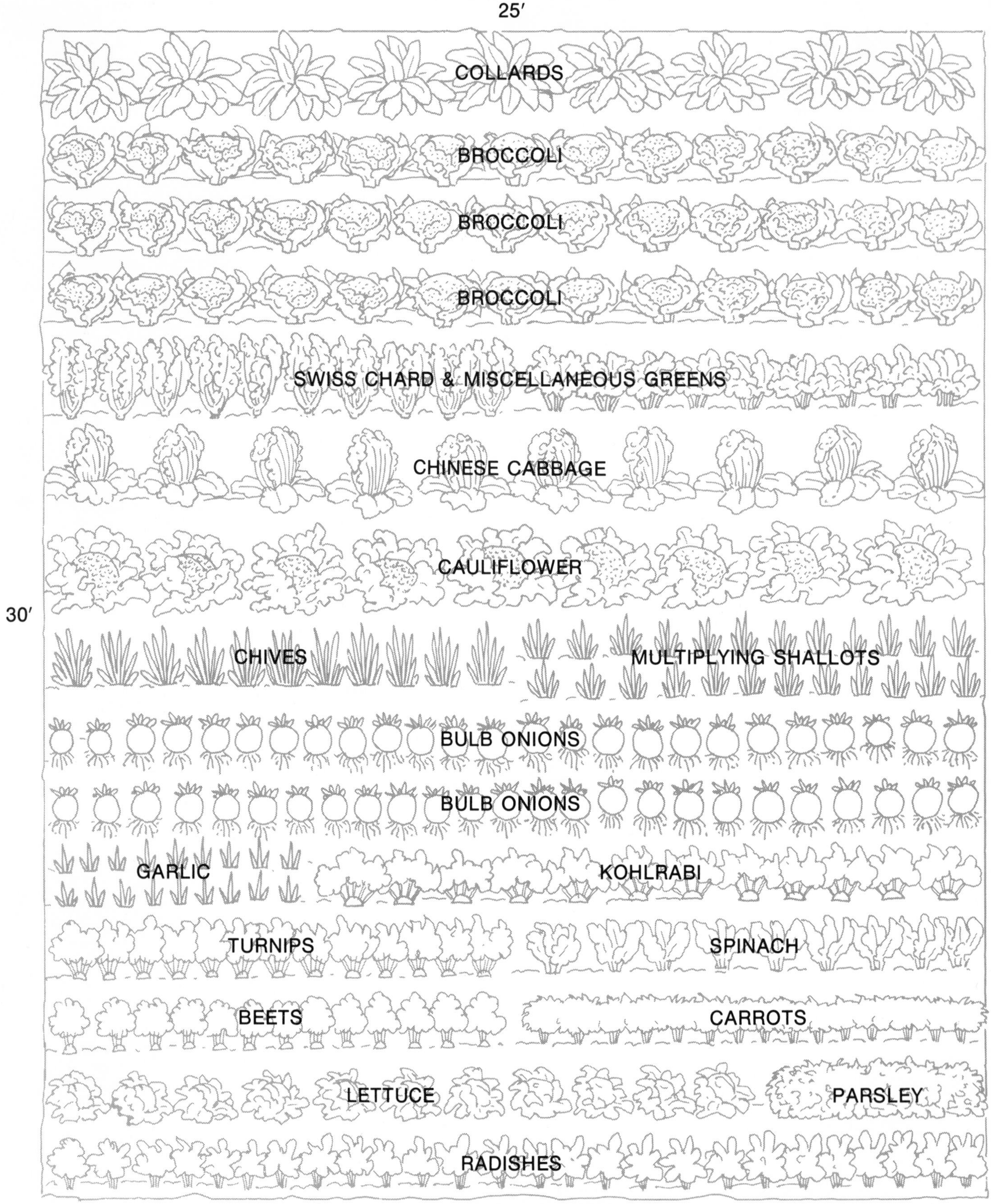

25'

COLLARDS

BROCCOLI

BROCCOLI

BROCCOLI

SWISS CHARD & MISCELLANEOUS GREENS

CHINESE CABBAGE

CAULIFLOWER

30'

CHIVES   MULTIPLYING SHALLOTS

BULB ONIONS

BULB ONIONS

GARLIC   KOHLRABI

TURNIPS   SPINACH

BEETS   CARROTS

LETTUCE   PARSLEY

RADISHES

Medium-size, cool season garden, 25' x 30'.

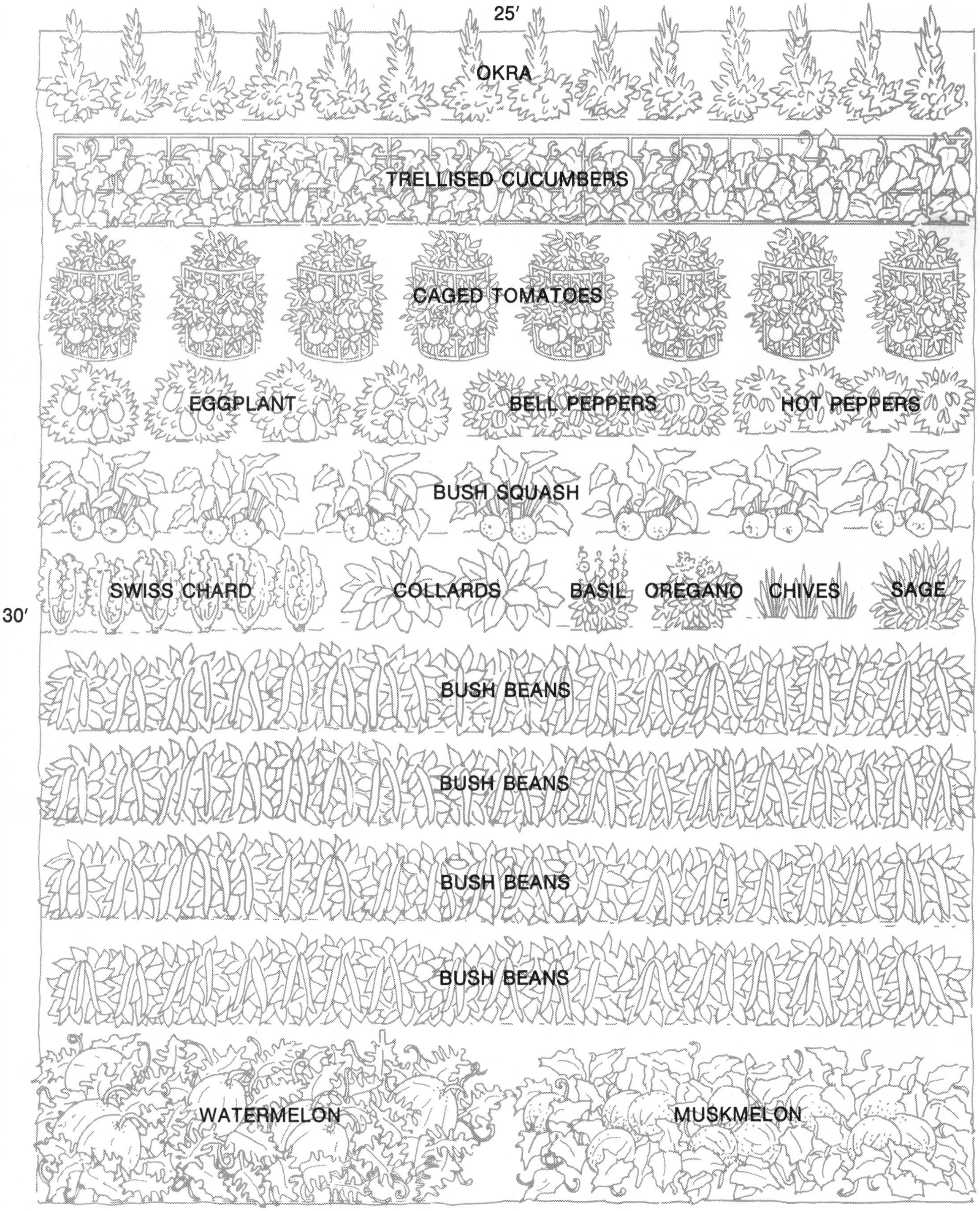

25'

OKRA

TRELLISED CUCUMBERS

CAGED TOMATOES

EGGPLANT   BELL PEPPERS   HOT PEPPERS

BUSH SQUASH

30'

SWISS CHARD   COLLARDS   BASIL   OREGANO   CHIVES   SAGE

BUSH BEANS

BUSH BEANS

BUSH BEANS

BUSH BEANS

WATERMELON   MUSKMELON

Medium-size, warm season garden, 25' x 30'.

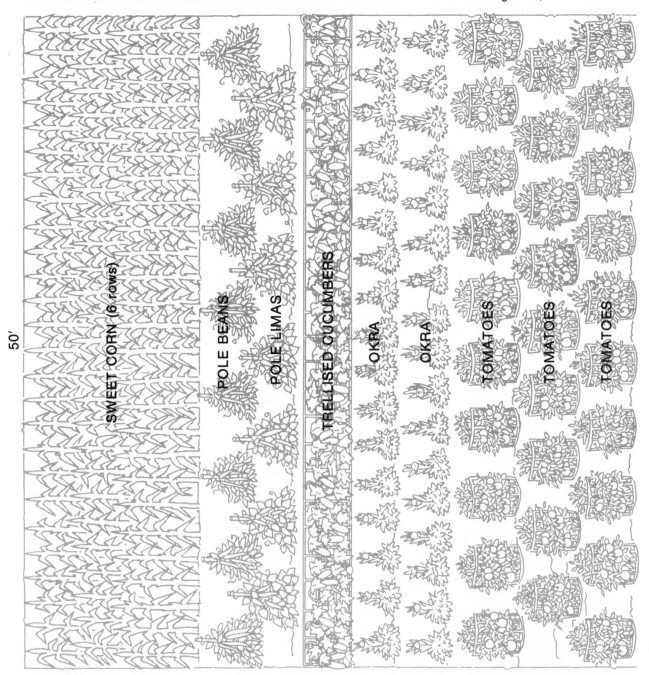

8'

PATIO TOMATOES   SQUASH (Gold Neck Hyb.)

4'

PEPPERS   SWISS CHARD (Burgundy var.)
(Yolo
Wonder   BASIL
var.)
                BUSH BEANS (Contender var.)

(Left) Small, warm season garden, 4' x 8'.

(Below and on opposite page) Large, warm season garden, 50' x 100'.

50'

SWEET CORN (6 rows)

POLE BEANS

POLE LIMAS

TRELLISED CUCUMBERS

OKRA

OKRA

TOMATOES

TOMATOES

TOMATOES

Cool Season Garden. The obvious difference between individual vegetable gardens will be a reflection of the gardeners' preferences for different vegetables. Not everybody likes collard greens, nor Swiss chard, nor parsley. Plant what you like, and if you only like one vegetable, devote the entire garden to it. Instead of collard greens, you can plant kale, including the edible flowering varieties, or you may prefer spinach. Oriental greens, such as mustard, Pac Choi, and Chinese cabbage, make good substitutes. You can substitute any other vegetable in the plan, as long as the substitute requires about the same amount of growing space. The same substitutions can be used

in place of broccoli and other members of the cabbage family.

Irish potatoes usually can't be planted in the South until February, so there's no reason short season crops such as lettuce can't be grown there until planting time.

Warm Season Vegetables. As with the cool season vegetables, the main differences in gardens will be in the types of vegetables you like to grow and eat. Once the corn is finished, either replant it (if you planted early you'll probably have time) or plant okra in its place. The pole beans and pole limas can be replaced with climbing okra (actually

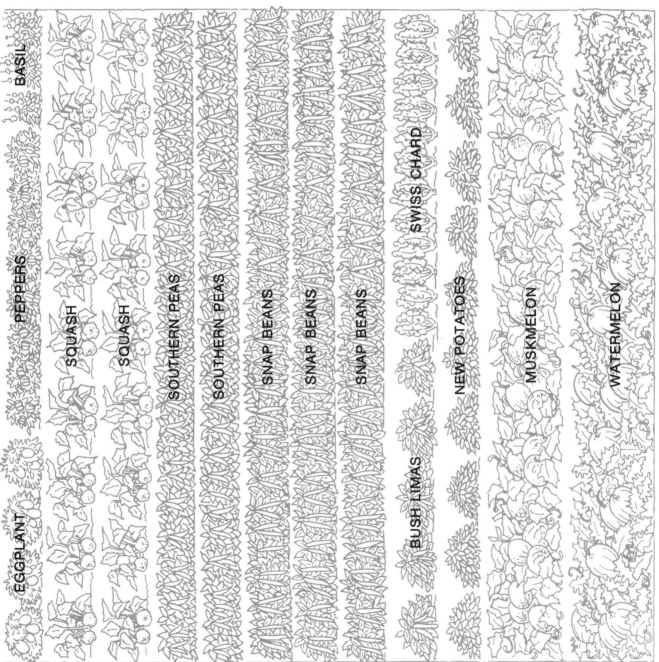

100'

a luffa gourd) or ornamental gourds. Jerusalem artichokes (Sun Chokes) planted in late spring will mature just about the time most areas in the South get their first frost.

If there's one time that it's hard to keep something going in the garden it's in mid-summer. Rather than plant the entire garden in okra or Jerusalem artichokes, you may have to let some of it rest temporarily, but by late summer you should be ready for a second crop of warm season vegetables like beans, tomatoes, peppers, squash, and cucumbers.

Vegetables to Stagger Plant. Vegetables that ripen uniformly and require prompt harvesting (some vegetables like carrots can remain in the ground a while) that can also be grown over a long season are best planted in successive rows or portions of a row every two weeks to avoid having an excess one week and nothing the next. Vegetables in this category include: snap beans, cabbage, Chinese cabbage, corn, kohlrabi, southern peas, radishes, and turnips.

Vegetables that Yield Over A Long Period of Time

Cool Season Vegetables

Collards
Kale
Leaf Lettuce
Mustard
Parsley
Turnip Greens

Warm Season Vegetables

Swiss Chard (this one also does well in cool weather)
Eggplant
Okra
Pepper
New Zealand Spinach
Malabar or Climbing Spinach

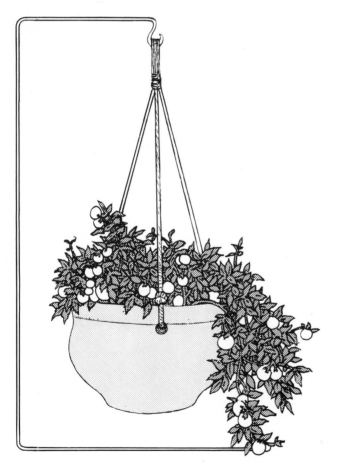

Cherry tomatoes in hanging baskets are attractive as well as practical.

Varieties for Container-Grown Vegetables

Tomatoes:	Patio, Pixie, Tiny Tim, Saladette, Stakeless, Atom
Peppers:	Yolo Wonder, Keystone Resistant Giant, Canape, (Hot) Red Cherry, Jalapeno
Eggplant:	Florida Market, Black Beauty, Long Tom
Squash:	Dixie, Gold Neck, Early Prolific Straightneck, (Green) Zucco, Diplomat, Senator
Leaf Lettuce:	Buttercrunch, Salad Bowl, Romaine, Dark Green Boston, Ruby, Bibb
Green Onions:	Beltsville Bunching, Crystal Wax, Evergreen Bunching
Green Beans:	Topcrop, Tendergreen, Contender, (Pole) Blue Lake, Kentucky Wonder
Radishes:	Cherry Belle, Scarlet Globe, (White) Icicle
Parsley:	Evergreen, Moss Curled
Cucumbers:	Burpless, Early-Pik, Crispy

Note: For additional information on variety selection, consult your county Extension agent or Extension horticulturist.

(Table courtesy of Texas Agricultural Extension Service Bulletin.)

container gardening

If you don't have a plot of ground to work up for a standard garden, or if nematodes or soil diseases such as wilt have discouraged you from working with the backyard soil, you might try growing vegetables in containers such as pots, planter boxes, plastic garbage cans, hanging baskets, or even in plastic soil bags. A number of vegeables can be grow in containers including: tomatoes, peppers, eggplant, cucumbers, lettuce, Swiss chard, green onions, collards, radishes, spinach, and turnips. Herbs sometimes grow better in containers than in the garden because of the better drainage and more controlled watering. Some good container herbs are: basil, borage, chervil, chives, sweet marjoram, oregano, mints, parsley, rosemary, sage, savory, tarragon, and thyme.

Use a commerically available potting soil, or prepare your own as suggested in the section on *Soil Preparation.* Because you'll be watering often, you'll need to fertilize every one to two weeks. The new controlled-release fertilizers (tiny time capsules of fertilizer) that continuously meter out fertilizer as you water will be helpful. Some gardeners like to fertilize at each watering with a very dilute solution of fertilizer. For fruiting crops like tomatoes and peppers, begin with a high-phosphorous formulation such as 12-55-6 and use one tablespoon per 3 gallons of water each time the plant needs watering. After fruit has set, use a higher nitrogen formulation such as 20-20-20 at the same dilution. Keep the fertilizer solution mixed up so it is always handy. Once a week, leach the soil out with plain water to reduce salt build-up. If you give plants the correct exposure (sun for most) and control pests, you should have good production.

The plastic bag your potting soil comes in makes a good planting container. Lay it down. Cut holes in the top, properly spaced for the vegetable you want to grow, punch a few pencil-thick holes in the side for drainage, and plant away.

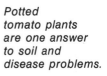

Potted tomato plants are one answer to soil and disease problems.

Planting Information for Growing Vegetables in Containers

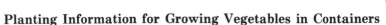

Crop	Number of Days for Germination	Number of Weeks to Optimum Age for Transplanting	General Size of Container	Amount of Light* Required	Number of Days from Seeding to Harvest
Beans	5-8	—	Medium	Sun	45-65
Cucumbers	5-8	3-4	Large	Sun	50-70
Eggplant	8-12	6-8	Large	Sun	100-130
Lettuce	6-8	3-4	Medium	Partial shade	45-60
Onions	6-8	6-8	Small	Partial shade	80-100
Parsley	10-12	—	Small	Partial shade	70-90
Pepper	10-14	6-8	Large	Sun	90-140
Radish	4-6	—	Small	Partial shade	20-60
Squash	5-7	3-4	Large	Sun	50-70
Tomato	7-10	5-6	Large	Sun	90-130

*All vegetables grow best in full sunlight, but those indicated will also do well in partial shade.

(Table courtesy of Texas Agricultural Extension Service Bulletin.)

Common Problems in Container Gardening

Symptoms	Cause	Corrective measures
Plants tall, spindly and unproductive	Insufficient light	Move container to area receiving more light
	Excessive nitrogen	Reduce feeding intervals
Plants yellowing from bottom, lack vigor, poor color	Excessive water	Reduce watering intervals Check for good drainage
	Low fertility	Increase fertility level of base solution
Plants wilt although sufficient water present	Poor drainage and aeration	Use mix containing higher percent organic matter; increase number of holes for drainage
Marginal burning or firing of the leaves	High salts	Leach container with tap water at regular intervals
Plants stunted in growth; sickly, purplish color	Low temperature	Relocate container to warmer area
	Low phosphate	Increase phosphate level in base solution
Holes in leaves, leaves distorted in shape	Insects	Use EPA-recommended insecticide
Plant leaves with spots; dead dried areas, or powdery or rusty areas	Plant diseases	Remove diseased areas where observed and use EPA-recommended fungicide

(Table courtesy of Texas Agricultural Extension Service Bulletin.)

Herbs make great hanging basket plants. This basket contains, from left center: thyme, Greek oregano, sweet marjoram and rosemary. In the center is a Mexican marigold mint.

USEFUL HERBS IN THE SOUTHERN GARDEN

In the South most herbs require good drainage. This usually means raised beds or growing in containers. Some, such as the mints, will tolerate poor drainage, but most need good drainage and full sun. More southern gardeners fail with herbs because they drown them than for any other reason.

Herb	Spring Planting	Fall Planting	Hardy	Annual	Perennial	Sun	Partial Shade	Shade	Height (inches)	Spread (inches)	Propagation from Seed	Propagation from Cuttings	Propagation from Divisions	Uses	Remarks
Basil	X			X		X	X		8-24	8-18	X†	X		Adds a clove-like flavor to tomato dishes. Also used with eggs, cheese, fish, poultry and in salads.	In addition to standard green varieties, there is a purple variety—Dark Opal. Basil is very easy to grow.
Borage	X			X		X	X		12-36	18-24	X			Young leaves are used to give a cucumber flavor to salads; also used in pickling.	Coarse plant, very attractive to bees. Easy to grow, can become a pest from reseeding.
Burnet	X	X	X		X	X			12-24	12-18	X†		X	Young leaves have a fresh cucumber flavor. Good for salads, ice drinks, herb butters and with cream cheese.	Good as a groundcover or in containers.
Chervil	X	X	X	X			X	X	12-24	12-18	X			Fine-textured foliage with a slight anise flavor. Enhances the flavor of other herbs.	Plant in the very early spring, in all but the deep South, in a rich organic soil.
Chives, Onion		X	X		X	X	X		12-18	10-15	X†		X	Chop up to use in dips, salads, cheese and egg dishes.	This is the tubular-leaved variety. Flowers are purple and appear before the white flowers of garlic chives.
Chives, Garlic		X	X		X	X	X		12-18	10-15	X†		X	Chop up to use in dips, salads, cheese and egg dishes.	Leaves are flat-bladed.
Coriander (Chinese Parsley, Cilantro)		X	X	X		X	X		18-24	12-18	X			Leaves have a strong, musty odor and are used sparingly in soup, especially with beans or in oriental dishes. Seeds are used in beans, soups, sausage and pastries.	
Dill	X*	X	X	X		X			24-48	18-30	X			Typically used to flavor pickles, but both seeds and leaves are also good in sauces, salad dressings, dips, with meats, and in breads.	Good drainage is important, but if growing conditions are good this plant can become a pest because of reseeding. A more compact variety is 'Bouquet'.

†Most common way
*Except in lower South
**Usually cultivated as an annual
***Actually a biennial

(Chart continued on next page)

USEFUL HERBS IN THE SOUTHERN GARDEN

In the South most herbs require good drainage. This usually means raised beds or growing in containers. Some, such as the mints, will tolerate poor drainage, but most need good drainage and full sun. More southern gardeners fail with herbs because they drown them than for any other reason.

Herb	Spring Planting	Fall Planting	Hardy	Annual	Perennial	Sun	Partial Shade	Shade	Height (inches)	Spread (inches)	Propagation from Seed	Propagation from Cuttings	Propagation from Divisions	Uses	Remarks
Fennel	X*	X	X		X**	X	X		36-48	30-48	X			Leaves and seeds have an anise or licorice flavor. Swollen basal stems are eaten like celery.	This plant requires about the same cultural treatment that dill does.
Garlic		X	X	X		X	X		18-36	12-18			X	Can be used in almost any non-dessert dish.	Excess garlic is better cleaned and frozen than dried.
Scented Geraniums	X				X	X	X		12-36	8-36	X	X		Many varieties are available, such as: rose, lemon, lime, nutmeg, apple, peppermint, almond, apricot, filbert and coconut.	Scented geraniums make excellent pot plants and many are also good in hanging baskets.
Lemon Balm	X	X	X		X	X	X		18-24	24-36		X	X	Good for teas or to add lemon flavor to cold drinks.	Very vigorous. This plant needs regular shearing to keep it in bounds.
Lemon Verbena	X				X	X			60″	48″	X	X		Imparts a delicate lemon fragrance or flavor to teas, ice drinks or potpourries.	Requires well-drained soil and protection in the winter.
Marjoram	X				X	X			12-24	12-24	X	X	X	Used for teas and with meat dishes. Marjoram is essentially a refined oregano.	This plant requires good drainage as well as full sun.
Mints	X	X	X		X	X	X	X	12-36	24-36		X	X	Many varieties are available, including: apple, spearmint, pineapple, peppermint and orange mint.	This is one herb that generally tolerates partial shade and poor drainage. Some varieties, such as orange mint, can become quite an invasive pest.
Oregano	X	X	X		X	X			18-30	24-36	X	X	X	This is the "pizza" herb. It is especially good in most highly seasoned dishes.	Oregano can be a very prolific herb if it is given sun and good drainage.

†Most common way
*Except in lower South
**Usually cultivated as an annual
***Actually a biennial

(Chart continued on next page)

USEFUL HERBS IN THE SOUTHERN GARDEN

In the South most herbs require good drainage. This usually means raised beds or growing in containers. Some, such as the mints, will tolerate poor drainage, but most need good drainage and full sun. More southern gardeners fail with herbs because they drown them than for any other reason.

Herb	Spring Planting	Fall Planting	Hardy	Annual	Perennial	Sun	Partial Shade	Shade	Height (inches)	Spread (inches)	Propagation from Seed	Propagation from Cuttings	Propagation from Divisions	Uses	Remarks
Parsley		X	X	X***		X	X		6-24	6-24	X			Parsley is reputed to counteract the effects of garlic—regardless, it is a delightful herb to munch on fresh from the garden.	Several forms are available. The plain-leaved varieties have more flavor but seem to bolt to seed more quickly in the spring than do the crinkle-leaved varieties.
Rosemary	X			X	X				18-60	24-48	X	X		Rosemary is a strong herb used sparingly with chicken and lamb—or brewed to make a tea.	Rosemary is often hardy in the lower South if given good drainage.
Sage	X		X		X	X			24-36	18-24	X	X		Sage is used in stuffings, and sausage and with lamb.	Good drainage is particularly important.
Summer Savory	X			X		X			18	12	X	X		Used to flavor vinegar and also with meats, eggs and beans.	Good drainage also required.
Winter Savory	X	X	X		X	X			6-12	12-16			X	Similar to above but a little stronger.	More of a spreading plant than above.
Tarragon	X	X	X		X		X		12-24	10-15			X	Tarragon has a slight anise flavor. It is used in vinegars, with salads, fish, cheese and in egg dishes.	The so-called Russian Tarragon is propagated by seed and is less desirable. This is not one of the easier herbs to grow in the South.
Thyme	X	X	X		X	X			4-12	6-18	X	X		Common thyme is typically used in beans. There are also other varieties, such as: caraway, silver thyme, lemon thyme, and woolly thyme.	Unless grown in a raised bed, thyme usually drowns in humid areas of the South.

†*Most common way*
Except in lower South
**Usually cultivated as an annual*
***Actually a biennial*

TRELLISING

Trellising is an excellent way to improve air circulation and thus reduce disease problems. It is also a great way to conserve space. Today's small home lot often necessitates space conservation when it comes to gardening. In fact, a space-saving technique is essential if you want to grow vining crops. Oriental gardeners, particularly the Japanese, are perhaps the most adept at growing a great many plants in a relatively small space because of limited land. Growing plants on trellises is the key to their success at this.

If you have a fence, use it. If you're planning to build a fence, consider one that you can put to good use growing plants. There's nothing wrong with wood—it's beautiful. Some sub-division building codes may even require wood fences, but they aren't the best for plants because the wood puts them in the shade some portion of the day (except on the south side). Chain-link fences may not be as attractive as wood, but they are great for growing plants on. Another, more attractive wire fence is a combination of welded wire with wood posts and stringers (see illustration #1). Popular techniques involve teepees, wire trellises, and A-frames (see illustrations #2, 3, and 4).

Many other techniques can be used, just experiment and use your ingenuity. Other good trellising methods include: wire cages (18 inches in diameter) made from 5-foot sections of 6-inch reinforcing wire. Plants are allowed to grow up the wire cylinder. Single poles (or old limbs) stuck into the ground can serve as climbing supports, and a nylon cord zig-zagged from the house eaves to the edge of a raised bed makes a good trellis.

Cord zig-zagged from the roof eaves of your house will make an ideal trellis for cucumbers.

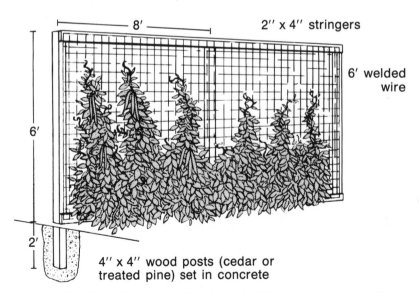

8′   2″ x 4″ stringers

6′ welded wire

6′

2′

4″ x 4″ wood posts (cedar or treated pine) set in concrete

Fence made with welded wire and 2 x 4 wood posts makes a good trellis.

Stakes attached to rafters with string support bean plants.

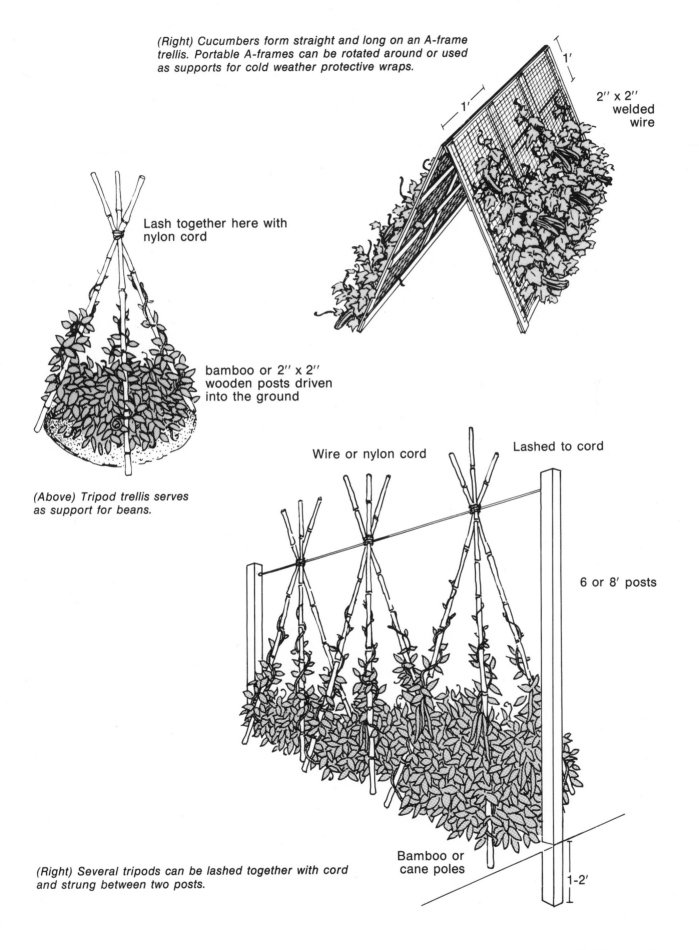

(Right) Cucumbers form straight and long on an A-frame trellis. Portable A-frames can be rotated around or used as supports for cold weather protective wraps.

1'

1'

2'' x 2'' welded wire

Lash together here with nylon cord

bamboo or 2'' x 2'' wooden posts driven into the ground

(Above) Tripod trellis serves as support for beans.

Wire or nylon cord

Lashed to cord

6 or 8' posts

Bamboo or cane poles

1-2'

(Right) Several tripods can be lashed together with cord and strung between two posts.

Trellising 15

What Makes a Good Soil?

A good soil should be loose, well-aerated, well-drained, and rich in organic matter and nutrients. Without these qualities a soil is a gardener's ball and chain; no matter how hard you try, your garden will never be fully successful.

Removing the Groundcover

When changing a lawn to a garden, flower bed, or shrub border, the first step is to eliminate the existing groundcover. To do this you could dig out the upper 6-12 inches of soil and haul if off, replacing it with a loamy topsoil. But before hauling off a poor soil, try adding it to the compost pile. Scatter the clods throughout the pile, and after you've turned it a couple of times, you'll find that it has been incorporated into the pile. Most soils, however, are suitable for use with a little improvement so removal of the soil should be considered as a last resort.

St. Augustine grass is easy to eliminate. Scraping the soil with a round pointed shovel will suffice. Bermuda grass is more difficult. It will regenerate rapidly from the roots, so scrape it, dig and turn it 6-12 inches deep, and then rototill. If you rototill several times, especially in the heat of the summer, the Bermuda will gradually die out.

Tilling

Whatever the original groundcover, you'll probably find a rototiller next to useless in unbroken clay soil. Turning the soil first with a spading fork will help the tiller dig in. It's best not to plow or till wet soil, but sometimes this is unavoidable. In high-rainfall areas of the South, if you wait for the soil to be just right you may end up not gardening. The requirement for proper soil moisture prior to cultivation is less of a problem in the small garden for several reasons. First, since you're using small equipment or handtools, there's less need for concern about compacting a wet soil

than if you were planting in a field and using heavy equipment. Also, you should be adding organic matter each year, and this makes the soil more workable.

DON'T run down to the rental store for a roto-tiller as your first step in soil preparation. All soils need additions of organic matter (pine bark, compost, rice hulls, etc.), but in the South even more is needed because the warmer soils burn up organic materials faster. The first step is to obtain sufficient organic matter to spread at least 2 inches over the garden plot area prior to roto-tilling. Scrape off the existing ground cover before you spread the organic matter, and if you have a tight clay soil, spade up the surface 6 to 8 inches, otherwise the roto-tiller is just going to bounce across the ground much as if you were trying to roto-till the sidewalk.

Help your rototiller do its job by turning unbroken clay soils with a spading fork beforehand.

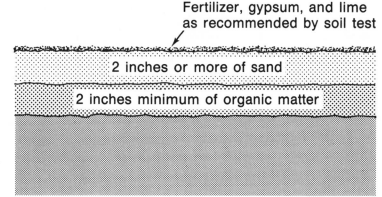

Fertilizer, gypsum, and lime
as recommended by soil test

2 inches or more of sand

2 inches minimum of organic matter

Before rototilling, spread out the materials you are going to add to the soil (as recommended by a soil test), along with 2 inches of organic matter and 2 inches of sand.

Loam

Finding the loamy topsoil is another problem. Loam consists of about 45% sand, 40% silt, and 15% clay, plus a lot of organic matter (5% or more of the total soil mass). You can't go to a soil store and have these specifications blended, so you have to take the dealer's word for it or go by feel. When you squeeze a handful of moist loam soil it should not compact so hard that it doesn't crumble readily when you touch it.

Clay and Sandy Soils

Clay soils, because they contain a greater proportion of small particles, will form a tight, sticky glob when wet. Sandy soils will crumble even more readily than loam because of the larger particles. Chances are you'll be starting with either clay or sandy soil. Fortunately, though they have different characteristics, both soils benefit from similar treatments—they both need plenty of organic matter.

Clay and Sandy Soils Compared

Nutrient Holding Capacity	Clay Soils High	Sandy Soils Low
Water Holding Capacity	High	Low
Aeration and Drainage Characteristics	Poor	Excellent

The size of soil particles determines the *texture* of the soil. An equally important factor is *soil structure*. This refers to the aggregation of the particles. If it has good structure, a clay soil may have as much important pore space as a loam soil because the tiny particles clump together. While it's often impractical to change the texture of a soil by adding larger soil particles, we can often change the structure of the soil by adding organic matter and gypsum.

ORGANIC MATTER

The most important soil amendment is organic matter. When mixed with clay soils it improves aeration and drainage; when mixed with sandy soils it improves moisture and nutrient-holding capacity. Some readily available organic materials are:

pine bark	rice hulls
peat moss	bagasse (sugar cane
compost	pulp)
	sawdust

well-rotted manure (manure that no longer has an odor or heats up)

If you've chosen to use the native soil as a base for the garden, spread at least 2 inches of organic matter over the soil. A full-sized ½-ton pickup truck holds about 2 to 3 cubic yards. So, for a garden 20 feet by 30 feet (600 square feet), you'll need two pickup loads to cover the 600 square feet 2 inches deep.

When incorporating organic materials, such as sawdust, into the soil, nitrogen may be temporarily tied up. The microorganisms (fungi and bacteria) that break down these materials rob the soil of nitrogen during the process. To compensate, compost the organic material first, or add nitrogen at the time of incorporation. The table on page 18 shows the amounts of nitrogen that are needed with pine bark, sawdust, and rice hulls.

soil activators

There is a plethora of "soil activators" on the market. Because these products are not generally offered as fertilizers they are not subject to regulation by state fertilizer laws. Most claim to stimulate microorganism activity in the soil, and some soil activator manufacturers claim that their products may improve physical properties of soils, increase fertilizer efficiency, increase the yield and quality of crops, correct soil "toxicities," and provide disease and insect resistance for crops.

These claims are based primarily on testimonials, with a notable lack of scientific data from agricultural universities or government agencies. The agricultural experiment stations in the states of Alabama, Florida, Georgia, Kentucky, Louisiana, North Carolina, Oklahoma, and Texas, along with the United States Department of Agriculture, recently (Aug. 1974) reported on two of these soil activators in Southern Cooperative Series Bulletin 189, *Effect of Two Soil Activators on Crop Yields and Activities of Soil Microorganisms in the Southern United States.*

The following information is adapted from the summary of this report. Only the brand names have been deleted.

1) Based on laboratory analyses, these products contain plant nutrients that are already common to soils. Based on manufacturer's recommendations, amounts of these elements added to soil would be low in relation to crop nutrient requirements.

2) Application of these products at recommended rates did not alter the number or activity of microorganisms that were naturally present in soil. The microorganism population in the products was considered to be too low for the products to be regarded as soil or plant inoculants.

3) The severity of cotton root rot was not reduced in greenhouse tests or in well-designed field trials where plots were of reasonable size for plant or yield evaluation.

4) Yields of grain sorghum, cotton, oats, Bermuda grass forage, soybeans, rice, peanuts, and tomatoes were not significantly increased with recommended applications of these products. Products were evaluated both with and without conventional fertilizers, on a wide variety of soils, and in irrigated and dryland fields. Where yields of succeeding crops were obtained, there was no indication of a delayed benefit.

The report goes on to say: "To significantly increase the activity of the microorganisms for more than a few hours several hundred pounds of organic tissue must be added to the soil. Usually, the commercial soil activators are applied at rates of only a few pounds per acre. Science has not yet discovered materials that are able to increase the activity of soil microorganisms when added to soils at low rates."

In short—spend your money on fertilizers and organic matter!!

Amounts of Nitrogen Needed with Pine Bark, Sawdust, Rice Hulls

4-6 Cubic Yards	Ammonium Sulfate (21-0-0) per cu yd	Houactinite (4% nitrogen)	Fish Meal (10% nitrogen) Blood Meal (12% nitrogen) per cu yd
Pine bark (untreated)	15 lbs	75 lbs	30 lbs
Sawdust	7½ lbs	37½ lbs	15 lbs
Rice hulls	3 lbs	15 lbs	6 lbs

Try to add these fertilizers at least a month or, if possible, a whole season prior to planting. Additional fertilizers will be required during the growing season.

MANURE

Everyone has their favorite manure. All manures are good, though there are slight differences, primarily in the percentages of nitrogen, phosphorous, and potassium they contain. Today, manure selection is a matter of taking what you can get. If it's fresh and heating, put it in the compost pile until it has cooled down a bit. Here are approximate percentages of some of the common manures:

	N%	P%	K%
Cattle	.7	.2	.5
Horse	.7	.3	.6
Sheep	.8	.3	.9
Poultry	1.1	.8	.5
Rabbitt	2.5	1.4	.6
Pig	.5	.3	.5

Those that are high in nitrogen, such as rabbit and poultry manure, should be used with caution to avoid burning.

Other organic amendments sometimes used in place of or in addition to manure for their fertilizer and soil improvement qualities are:

	nitrogen %	phosphorous %	potassium %
Coffee grounds	2.08	.32	.67
Cottonseed	3.15	1.25	1.15
Fish Scrap	7.76	13.00	.38
Seaweed	1.68	.75	4.93
Wood Ashes	—	1.00—2.00	4.00—10.00

OTHER SOIL AMENDMENTS

Working 2 inches of sand into a clay soil (4 cu yds per 600 sq ft), is also beneficial. Although sharp sand is often recommended, bank sand (pit sand), as long as it doesn't contain salt, also works well. It is finer than sharp sand, but if you combine 2 inches of this sand with 2 inches of organic matter, the results are excellent.

Some gardeners have prepared a clay soil using sand alone, but 4 inches of sand or more will be needed. If given the choice of only organic matter or sand, by all means choose the organic matter.

For clay soils, you may want to spread 5-10 pounds of gypsum and 2-3 pounds of 12-24-12 or a similar analysis fertilizer per 100 square feet. For acid-loving plants, incorporate 1 to 2 pounds of sulfur or iron sulfate (copperas). See the pH chart on page 26. 12-24-12 is a good general fertilizer for sandy soils. A similar amount of 16-20-0 is usually sufficient for clay soils because these soils usually contain ample potassium. If tomatoes, peppers or other fruit-bearing crops are to be planted, a good garden soil will often need only the addition of superphosphate (0-20-0) as a preplant incorporation. Once the plants have produced fruit an inch in diameter, sidedressing with nitrogen will be necessary. Ammonium sulfate (21-0-0) can be used for sidedressing at the rate of ½-¾ pound per 100 feet of row, approximately 1 tablespoon per 2 feet of row.

Fertilizers

In applying fertilizer to home lawns, gardens, flower beds and compost piles, it is often necessary to convert suggested rates into amounts for smaller areas or for row application. This information is contained in Tables 1, 2, and 3.

To fertilize properly it is necessary to understand what makes up a fertilizer, especially if you have to substitute a different analysis. The label on the fertilizer bag shows the percentages of nitrogen, phosphorus, and potassium. For example, a 12-12-12 fertilizer contains 12% each of nitrogen (N), phosphorus (P), and potassium (K) respectively. A 50-pound bag contains 6 pounds of each nutrient or 18 pounds total. A 10-6-4 fertilizer would contain 20 pounds of nutrients. The remainder of the fertilizer is made up of other elements, such as oxygen, hydrogen, etc., which are chemically combined in the sources of nutrients used. Some fertilizers may contain an inert filler as well.

Fertilizer Conversion Table 1.
Conversion from Pounds Per Acre Into Weights for Small Areas

Rates per acre (lbs)	Lbs per	
	1000 sq ft	100 sq ft
100	2½	¼
200	5	½
400	9	1
800	18½	2
1000	23	2½
Manure, leaves and straw		
8000 (4 tons)	200	20
16000 (8 tons)	400	40

Fertilizer Conversion Table 2.
Conversion from Area Rate to Linear Row

Rates per		Row width		
1000 sq ft	100 sq ft	3 ft	2 ft	1 ft
Lbs	Lbs	Lbs per 100 ft of row		
5	½	1½	1	½
10	1	3	2	1
20	2	6	4	2
30	3	9	6	3
40	4	12	8	4
50	5	15	10	5

Fertilizer Conversion Table 3.
Conversion from Area Rate to Per Plant Basis

Rates per 100 sq ft	Spacings		
	5 x 5 ft	2½ x 2½ ft	2½ x 1½ ft
Lbs	Oz * per plant		
½	2	1	½
1	4	2	1
2	8	4	2
3	12	6	3
4	16	8	4
5	20	10	5

*1 oz. = 2 tbsp.

Fertilizer Conversion Table 4.
Factors for Converting Suggested Rates When Substituting A Different Analysis Fertilizer

Suggested analysis	Analysis to be substituted	Rate conversion factor*
12-12-12	20-20-20	.6
	17-17-17	.7
	16-6-12	.8
	15-15-15	.8
	13-13-13	1
	12-6-6	1
	10-5-5	1.2
	10-6-4	1.2
10-20-10	5-10-5	2
	5-15-5	2
	6-12-6	1.7
	12-24-12	.85
	15-30-15	.65
10-20-20	12-24-24	.85
	15-30-30	.65

*Multiply times rate for suggested analysis. Example: want to substitute 20-20-20 for 15 pounds 12-12-12. 15 x .6 = 9 pounds 20-20-20 needed.

Tables adapted from Fertilizer Conversion Tables, Texas Agricultural Extension, Service, Texas A&M University System.

Since many different fertilizers are sold but the selection from a given store is limited, substitutions are often necessary. Generally, the basis for substitution is the amount of nitrogen in the fertilizer. Substitutions can be made as long as enough fertilizer is used to meet plant food requirements, but not enough applied to injure germinating seeds, seedlings, or growing plants.

A complete fertilizer contains nitrogen, phosphorus, and potassium. Some common analyses and possible substitutions are presented in Table 4. The factors for converting from a standard analysis to a desired substitute are listed. For example, a 13-13-13 is so near a 12-12-12 that the same rate can be used, but only .8 as much 15-15-15 would be required to supply the same amount of nutrients as a 12-12-12. If 15 pounds of 12-12-12 per 1,000 square feet is suggested, the same amount of N, P, and K would be supplied by 12 pounds of 15-15-15 (15 x .8 = 12).

If the soil has been spaded prior to putting out added materials, it will be a fairly easy task to run the tiller through it. Two to three weeks after you've prepared the soil is usually the best time to have the soil tested—especially if this is the first time you've worked it. By then the soil microorga-

nisms will have begun using the organic matter you've added, and the fertilizer nutrients will have dissolved and spread out in the soil. You may also want to test the soil prior to adding soil amendments just to know what you started with. Almost all states have an Agricultural Extension Service. Contact your local County Extension Agent for more information about soil testing facilities in your state.

Gypsum. Is gypsum a miracle worker that magically turns tight clay soils into loams? Hardly. Gypsum benefits the soil by replacing sodium with calcium. This is beneficial because sodium causes the soil particles to compact, thus reducing pore space, aeration, and damaging soil structure in general. When calcium replaces sodium the particles aggregate into many tiny clumps, thus improving soil structure.

A watering can with the diffusing nozzle removed makes an excellent device for applying a sidedressing of fertilizer, as this gardener is doing on his potatoes.

If sodium isn't a problem, if your drainage is too poor to facilitate washing the sodium out of the soil, or if the irrigation water contains plenty of sodium, gypsum will be of little help, and adding gypsum can certainly be overdone.

Potting mixture. For a soil-less soil to fill pots or wooden planter boxes in a mini-garden, try the following: To 1 bushel each of vermiculite and shredded peat moss (8 dry gallons = 1 bushel/plastic garden bags come in a 7 to 10 gallon size), add 1¼ cups of ground or dolomitic limestone, ½ cup of superphosphate, and ½ cup of 12-24-12 fertilizer. Mix thoroughly and add water so that the soil holds its shape when squeezed.

COMPOSTING

Most of the information on composting sounds about the same: begin with a 6-inch layer of organic matter, cover this with 1 inch of soil, continue layering soil and organic matter until the pile is 4-6 feet high, form the top of the pile into a dish-shape so that it will catch water and, of course, add water. There's nothing wrong with these recommendations, but they're based on an ideal situation which most of us don't have. The two essential characteristics of a good compost are:

Uniformity—few, if any, of the original ingredients should be recognizable. Instead, compost should be dark, crumbly, and it should have a good earthy odor.

Freedom from heating—The capacity to heat up, even if the compost is turned and moistened, should be lost. This stage should have been preceded by several periods of heating during the initial composting process. If no heat has ever been produced, you probably don't have compost.

How do you make compost that fits the above description? If you know the following basic processes, you can develop your own technique for making compost.

1) You need *organic matter*. You can use what you have, or you can be resourceful and incorporate all kinds of organic materials such as your neighbors' leaves and lawn clippings that are normally considered waste products or trash. If you decide to use only what your household produces, you'll probably have kitchen garbage, lawn clippings, and some leaves. In this case, you'll find that getting enough organic matter to make a typical compost pile will be difficult, so you may want to try an alternative method of composting. One technique uses a garbage can or plastic bag. It has one major drawback—the lack of oxygen inherent in this system causes the compost to have a strong odor. Also, it will probably take longer for the materials to break down, but when aired out the end result is about the same as compost made the conventional way.

(Text continued on page 23)

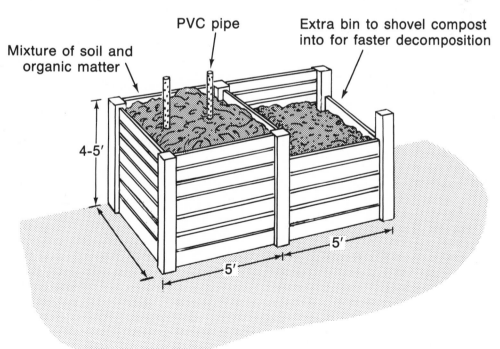

Mixture of soil and organic matter

PVC pipe

Extra bin to shovel compost into for faster decomposition

4-5'

5'

5'

Compost pile with perforated PVC pipe for aeration.

essential soil elements

Each essential nutrient is involved in one or more metabolic processes affecting plant growth. Therefore, symptoms resulting from a reduced level in these processes cause visual evidence of deficiency called "symptoms." Some important functions and a description of nutrient deficiency symptoms for the 13 mineral nutrients are presented in this discussion.

Nitrogen

Function. Nitrogen is needed for amino acids, the building blocks of protein. Nitrogen also is found in the chlorophyll molecule which gives plants their green color and photosynthetic capacity.

Deficiency symptoms. The first evidence of nitrogen deficiency is a light green color, indicating reduced chlorophyll formation. The older leaves begin to yellow, starting at the tip. An inverted "V" frequently forms as yellowing proceeds down the midrib of the leaf of a grass-type plant. Older leaves become deficient first, resulting from the translocation of nitrogen to young tissue. Nitrogen deficiency symptoms often are observed on nonlegume crops since most soils are low in this nutrient and fertilization is often inadequate.

Phosphorus

Function. Phosphorus is necessary for the utilization of energy in plant metabolism and also is required in cell division. Phosphorus is necessary for the photosynthetic reaction which transforms the energy of sunlight into carbohydrates.

Deficiency symptoms. Reduced growth, thin stalks, small leaves and delayed maturity are signs of a deficiency. In severe deficiency, there is a dark purple cast to leaves and stems. Phosphorus deficiency is difficult to confirm, because of a lack of distinct leaf symptoms.

Potassium

Function. Potassium is needed for protein and carbohydrate formation and the activation of specific enzymes. Potassium is associated with the water relationship in plants. It has not been identified in chemical combinations in plants, but is considered a regulator of essential reactions necessary for metabolism and growth.

Deficiency symptoms. Reductions in yield and quality of fruit and seeds are signs of deficiency. With corn or sorghum, leaf tips dry up. This condition moves down the leaf margins as the deficiency develops. Under extreme deficiency, the entire leaf turns brown and dies. Potassium moves from older to younger leaves as deficiencies, hence the deficiency develops on the older leaves first. Alfafa and clover display characteristic white dots near their margin when potassium is deficient.

Calcium

Function. Calcium is a component of the cell wall and is necessary for cell elongation and division.

Deficiency symptoms. Poor root growth and roots turning black and rotting are indications of calcium deficiency. In severe cases, the growing point dies. Leaf tips may become gelatinous. Symptoms develop on young tissue because calcium is not translocated. Calcium deficiency symptoms seldom are seen under field conditions, because of secondary effects such as high acidity.

Magnesium

Function. Magnesium is a component of chlorophyll and is necessary for amino acid and fat synthesis. Magnesium also affects the viability of seeds.

Deficiency symptoms. A crimson-reddish color in the lower leaves of cotton with green veins is a sign of deficiency. This can be an orange-yellow in corn, potatoes, cabbage and other crops. Magnesium is translocated, so symptoms will be found first in older leaves.

Sulfur

Function. Sulfur is a component of some amino acids which are in most protein molecules. It is needed in the formation of new cells and for chlorophyll.

Deficiency symptoms. Leaves get smaller and turn light green. Stems are thin and woody. Leaves die only in extreme cases, although death may result in the seedling stage. This generally affects the entire plant.

(Continued)

essential soil elements

Boron

Function. Boron is essential for pollen, seed and cell wall formation. The exact role is not well defined.

Deficiency symptoms. A deficiency of boron generally stunts plants. The growing point and young leaves are affected first, and the growing point dies, indicating that boron is not readily translocated. Alfafa acquires reddish coloration; celery stems are distorted and roots develop black spots. Sweet potatoes, apples and some other fruits and vegetables develop corky spots. Peanuts develop a dark discoloration in the kernel.

Molybdenum

Function. Molybdenum activates the enzyme nitrate reductase which reduces nitrates to ammonium in the plant. M_0 is essential for nodule formation (symbiotic fixation of nitrogen) by legumes.

Deficiency symptoms. Grain crops are yellow-green, usually being more pronounced in the younger leaves. With citrus, leaves develop water-soaked areas called "yellow spots." It frequently appears as a nitrogen deficiency in legumes, reflecting its role in nitrogen fixation and nitrate reduction. When nitrogen is applied in such cases, the leaves turn green. Cauliflower displays characteristic "whiptail" as a result of molybdenum deficiency.

Iron

Function. Iron is a catalyst in the formation of chlorophyll and acts as an oxygen carrier within the plant.

Deficiency symptoms. Signs of a deficiency are a pale green color with a sharp distinction between green veins and yellow interveinal tissues. Under severe deficiency, the entire plant turns yellow-to-bleached white. Iron deficiency occurs in the youngest tissue first, since it is not readily translocated within the plant. Grain sorghum is a good indicator crop for iron deficiency.

Manganese

Function. Manganese activates enzymes involved in chlorophyll formation and oxidation-reduction systems within the plant.

Deficiency symptoms. Deficiency appears in the younger leaves first. Yellowing between veins and sometimes a series of brownish-black specks occur. With small grains, grayish areas appear near the base of the younger leaves. Soybeans are a good indicator crop.

Chlorine

Little is known about the exact role of chlorine except that it is essential for plant growth. Only artificially induced deficiences have been observed.

Reprinted, with permission, from *Texas Soil Fertility*, published by the Texas Agricultural Extension Service in cooperation with Texas Plant Food Institute.

COMPOSTING (continued).

A variation of the garbage can technique produces a more typical compost without the strong odor. It requires the following: a garbage can with holes drilled into the bottom and a 1-2 inch layer of gravel over the holes. Placing the can on bricks further facilitates drainage and improves aeration. Leaving the lid off and placing several plastic tubes (with holes drilled in the side) into the compost should further improve aeration if odor becomes a problem.

Another method utilizes small amounts of organic matter (which really isn't composting in the strictest sense). Dig small holes in the garden or flower bed and gradually fill these with layers of organic matter, usually the day's kitchen garbage. As each layer is put in cover it with a little soil. When the hole fills up, plant a plant in it and dig another hole. The disadvantage of this system is that no appreciable heat is formed, and disease, insect, and weed organisms are not destroyed. However, if you're using kitchen garbage none of these pests will be present in very high concentrations.

2) You need *nitrogen*. If your organic matter source is high in nitrogen, you don't have to worry about adding supplemental nitrogen. Green grass clippings, kitchen garbage (free of paper), and manure usually have plenty of nitrogen. Dry leaves, paper, sawdust, hay, and similar materials will require additional nitrogen. The safest way to add extra nitrogen is with an organic fertilizer such as blood meal, manure, or treated sewage sludge (raw sludge should be used only on compost destined for the flower bed). Inorganic fertilizers can be used, but strong concentrations may temporarily kill the organisms necessary for decomposition. About 1½ cups of 12-24-12 or similar analysis fertilizer per bushel of organic matter is adequate. Be sure to water in thoroughly any nitrogenous materials added to the pile or garbage can.

Limestone is often suggested as an added material for the compost pile. If a neutral or slightly alkaline compost is desired, add dolomitic limestone (contains magnesium as well as calcium) at the rate of ⅔ cup per bushel of organic matter. If your soil is already neutral or alkaline this really isn't necessary, and the addition of lime will result in a loss of nitrogen as ammonia.

Other additives, such as rock phosphate, wood ashes, and granite dust (the latter two are high in potash), may be incorporated although they are not absolutely necessary. Most composting materials have adequate supplies of these minerals. If a soil test indicates your soil is low in phosphorous or potassium (potash), you can increase the concentration of these elements by adding the previously mentioned materials during the composting process.

3) *Water* is also needed. Even in the South you will probably have to water the compost pile. If it dries out, microorganism activity comes to a screeching halt. On the other hand, if it gets too wet it smells bad because air is excluded.

4) As the last statement implies, *oxygen* is needed for odorless compost. Oxygen content depends not only on the amount of water in the pile but also on the size of the composting particles—if they're too small they compact and can become malodorous; if they're too large the compost dries out too quickly and the microorganisms die. If the particles are too large you can use a shredder specially made to grind compost. Some gardeners simply run over it several times with a lawnmower. If particles are too small add some coarser materials like leaves, or turn the pile more often. Some build their compost around poles stuck in the ground, removing the poles when the pile is built, leaving air passages through the compost. Plastic pipe (with holes in the side) can be left in the pile permanently.

5) *Turning* the pile in addition to supplying oxygen, also ensures that all the ingredients get adequate exposure to high temperatures. As you turn the pile the outside materials are thrown into the center, where temperatures rise and a better "kill" of weed seeds, diseases, and insects is effected. Generally, the more frequently you turn the pile the quicker the compost will be ready. Turning every three or four days is hard work, so most gardeners turn the pile only once, about a month after building it, and settle for compost that's ready in three months instead of three weeks.

6) For the pile to build up heat, it must be large enough to *insulate* the center of the pile. The usual dimensions are 4-6 feet wide, 4-6 feet high, and as long as necessary. Covering the pile with a sheet of black plastic will help retain heat. A retaining structure built from old lumber, concrete blocks, chicken wire, etc. will keep the pile in place.

Whatever systen you use, you'll find that compost is a key to successful vegetable gardening.

Turning a compost pile helps speed decomposition of the organic matter by increasing the concentration of oxygen.

tools you'll need

Most people have a round-pointed shovel, a hoe, a rake and probably a hand trowel around the house. These tools will usually be adequate for your first garden, but you'll eventually want a spading fork and a sturdy wheel barrow. A rototiller shouldn't be your first purchase. They're easy to rent and the cost of owning one is hard to justify for the first garden.

Also, you'll want two sturdy 18-inch stakes and a roll of nylon cord to use in laying out plots, plus garden hoses, a fertilizer spreader (the hand type works well for a small garden), and spray equipment. Although a hoze-on sprayer will be fairly good for applying pesticides, a pressurized sprayer is much more accurate at applying the spray where it needs to be (usually on the underside of the leaves where insects feed), and it's also more accurate at applying the recommended concentration of ingredient.

Spading fork

Rake

Garden hose

Fertilizer spreader

Round pointed shovel

Hand trowel

Hoe

Wheelbarrow

WHAT'S pH?

Soil acidity or alkalinity is measured by a factor called pH. An extremely alkaline soil would have a pH of 14.0. Actually, no such soil exists, as soils with a pH greater than 8.0 would be detrimental to plant growth. A neutral soil has a pH of 7.0, and an acid soil has a pH of less than 7.0. A soil having a pH lower than 5.0 would be too acidic for most plant growth.

Clay soils are usually neutral to alkaline in pH, and sandy soils are often acid in reaction, except in arid regions or in areas where salt is present in the soil. Most plants grow best in soil having a pH between 6.5 and 7.0. Soil pH is important in that it affects the availability of the various soil nutrients as indicated in the bar graph.

Changing the pH of a soil, especially a clay soil, is not easy and it's usually quite slow. Clay soils have a great buffering capacity, or an ability to

VEGETABLES

Crop	pH Range
Asparagus	6.0 - 7.0
Beans	6.0 - 7.5
Beans, Lima	5.5 - 7.5
Beets	6.0 - 7.5
Broccoli	6.0 - 8.0
Brussel sprouts	6.0 - 7.5
Cabbage	6.0 - 8.0
Cantaloupe	6.0 - 8.0
Carrot	6.0 - 7.5
Cauliflower	5.5 - 7.5
Cucumber	5.5 - 8.0
Eggplant	5.5 - 7.5
Irish potato (For control of scab)	4.8 - 5.4
Irish potato (For plant growth and yield)	5.5 - 7.5
Lettuce	6.0 - 7.5
Mustard	5.5 - 6.5
Okra	6.0 - 7.5
Onion	6.0 - 8.0
Parsley	6.0 - 8.0
Peas	6.0 - 8.0
Pepper	5.5 - 7.0
Pumpkin	5.5 - 7.0
Radish	6.0 - 8.0
Spinach	6.0 - 8.0
Soybeans	5.5 - 7.5
Sugar beets	7.0 - 8.0
Sweet corn	6.0 - 7.5
Sweet potato	5.0 - 7.0
Tomato	6.0 - 7.5
Turnip	5.5 - 7.0
Velvet beans	6.0 - 7.0
Watermelon	6.0 - 7.5

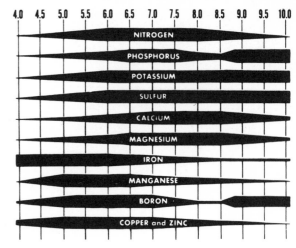

Availability of nutrients (pH range). Bar represents degree of availability.

the reading you get). Place this soil in a small container along with 50 cc of distilled water. Stir periodically over a 5-minute period and allow the soil to settle to the bottom of the container. Use Nitrazene paper to test the pH. This paper is readily available in most drug stores.

Instructions for Taking Soil Samples

Soil tests are only as accurate as the samples on which they are made. Therefore, proper collection of samples is extremely important. Take at least one separate composite sample for each soil type or soil condition. Soil variations can be due to texture (size of particles), slope, color, drainage, or past treatment. For example, if one area is sandy and another is heavier, take two separate composite samples. (*Note:* If sample is taken from problem area, such as bare spots in lawn, it is necessary that one composite sample come from the problem area, and one composite sample come from the surrounding good area. See note on plant diseases below.)

For a composite sample, obtain at least ten samples from the area, put in a clean container (bucket, sack, etc.) and mix thoroughly. Take out about 1 pint. Place in a clean container, such as an ice cream carton or paper sack, and submit for testing.

Use a garden trowel or spade to take a sample. Dig a V-shaped hole, then take a ½-inch slice from the smooth side of the hole. Place in a bucket and repeat in about ten places. Take samples to a depth of 6 inches in flower beds and gardens and 4 inches in lawns. A soil probe or soil auger can also be used. Label each sample with number and name.

resist change. Sandy soils, however, particularly acid sandy soils, can easily be improved by adding lime. Lime should only be added, however, as recommended by a soil test.

A relatively simple and accurate means of testing the soil pH is to place one tablespoon of air-dried soil (be sure to handle the soil with clean tools and not with your hands, they may influence

(Text continued on page 28)

raised bed plantings

Trying to make tight, wet soils drain well enough to grow vegetables can be frustrating. Many southern gardeners are finding that a better solution, at least for some vegetables and herbs, is to construct raised beds. In addition to improved drainage, the looser soil mixes used to fill these raised planting beds makes it easier to grow root crops.

Beds can be constructed out of railroad ties, 2-by-10 boards of treated pine or cedar (which is rot-resistant), or anything else you can use to retain the soil 6-12 inches deep.

The soil mix is the hardest thing to find for a reasonable price in an adequate quantity. One part soil, one part sand, and one part organic matter (pine bark, peat moss, or compost) makes a great mix, but buying those ingredients for any but the smallest area can be expensive. Some people have good luck filling the beds with well-rotted manure. Stable litter, with lots of straw or wood chips, decomposed to compost makes an excellent soil mix.

Raised beds require more water, but it's easier to add water than it is to drain it. More fertilizer is also needed for raised beds, but this, too, is less of a problem than trying to wash excess fertilizer out of a poorly drained soil. Using organic fertilizers that are less soluble will help reduce the required frequency of fertilization.

This raised bed with patio tomatoes is an easy way to get around poor drainage problems.

Be sure to keep a record of the area from which the samples came.

Note on Plant Diseases. When grasses, vegetables, or flowers die it is seldom due to a lack of soil fertility. So, with these symptoms, a soil test will be of little value. If difficulties in plant growth appear to be due to diseases see your County Extension Agent for diagnosis and further information. (Adapted from Soil Sample Information Sheet, Texas Agricultural Extension Service, Texas A&M University System.)

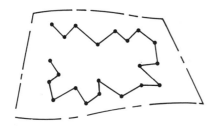

Step 1.
For a composite sample, obtain at least 10 samples from the area, put in a clean container (bucket, sack, etc.) and mix thoroughly. Take out about 1 pint. Place in a clean container, such as an ice cream carton or paper sack, and submit for testing.

Step 2.
To take a sample, use a garden trowel or spade. Dig a V-shaped hole, then take a ½-inch slice from the smooth side of the hole. Place in a bucket and repeat in about ten places. Take samples to a depth of 6 inches in flower beds and gardens and 4 inches in lawns. A soil probe or soil auger also can be used.

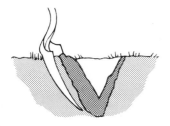

Step 3.
Label each sample with number and name. Be sure to keep a record of the area from which the samples came. Fill out the opposite side of this sheet as completely as possible and submit with the sample to the Soil Testing Laboratory.

Planting, Thinning, Watering, Mulching

Novice gardeners more often plant seed too deep than too shallow. (See the Planting Chart, page 50.) Proper planting depth is especially important when gardening in a clay soil or when planting small seed. Lettuce seed, for instance, must have light to germinate. If planted too deep the light can't reach it and it may not even sprout. If it does sprout, the distance up through the soil may be too great for the seedling to emerge and grow successfully. Small-seeded vegetables such as lettuce are best planted by scattering the seed over the soil and lightly raking it in. Follow with sprinkler irrigation, and don't allow the soil to dry out until the seedlings emerge. Of course, don't keep them standing in water either.

Seed is relatively cheap so don't skimp when you're planting. Thinning is not easy. It's hard work, and it's sometimes hard to convince yourself to pull up (actually it's better to snip off) healthy young seedlings. If you don't thin, however, you'll soon see that you should have. Plants will be stunted and overall production reduced. Do your thinning in two stages; that way if the bugs help with the thinning chores all will not be lost.

In most areas of the South, planting is best done on ridges. This lessens the problem of too much soil

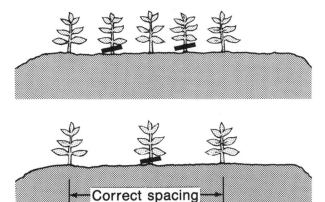

Thinning is best done in two stages—the bugs may help you.

Average Frost Dates for Southern Cities

Last Spring Frost	First Fall Frost
Mobile, Alabama-February 17	December 12
Montgomery, Alabama-March 3	November 19
Hot Springs, Arkansas-March 30	November 6
Little Rock, Arkansas-March 17	November 13
Ft. Smith, Arkansas-March 21	November 10
Jacksonville, Florida-February 15	December 11
Tampa, Florida-January 13	December 27
Tallahassee, Florida-February 25	December 4
Savannah, Georgia-February 28	November 28
Athens, Georgia-April 2	November 5
Atlanta, Georgia-March 23	November 9
Tifton, Georgia-March 6	November 17
Baton Rouge, Louisiana-February 24	November 20
New Orleans, Louisiana-February 20	December 9
Farmerville, Louisiana-March 28	November 1
Natchez, Mississippi-March 13	November 13
Biloxi, Mississippi-February 26	November 29
Ardmore, Oklahoma-March 21	November 10
Oklahoma City, Oklahoma-March 28	November 7
Grennville, S. Carolina-March 27	November 10
Pinopolis, S. Carolina-March 5	November 25
Lufkin, Texas-March 15	November 17
Gainesville, Texas-March 27	November 8
Dallas, Texas-March 18	November 17
El Paso, Texas-March 21	November 14
Galveston, Texas-January 21	December 28
Lubbock, Texas-April 12	November 3
Houston, Texas-February 10	December 8
Brownsville, Texas-January 30	December 26

(Taken from the U.S.D.A. Handbook of Agriculture, *Climate and Man*.)

moisture during heavy rains. If water excludes oxygen from the soil, plant roots can't absorb the water, and the plants wilt as if suffering from a drought.

HOW TO BE THE FIRST ON YOUR BLOCK WITH VEGETABLES

When buying transplants for the garden, try to select dark green, stocky plants rather than tall spindly ones. Should you be forced to purchase the

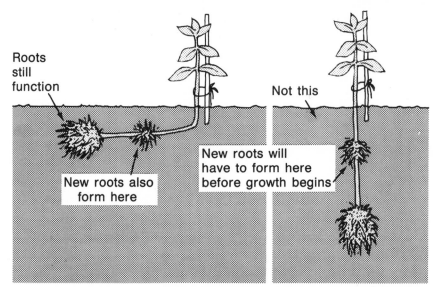

Roots still function

New roots also form here

New roots will have to form here before growth begins

Not this

Planting transplants in a shallow trench allows old roots to function while new ones develop.

latter type, plant them in a trench rather than in a post hole.

Starter Solution. A starter solution can be made by mixing 1 tablespoon of 12-24-12 in one gallon of water. Use ½ to 1 pint of this solution around each plant as it is set out.

The earlier you can get plants growing vigorously in the garden the more production you can expect. This is especially true with tomatoes, cucumbers, squash, cantaloupes, and watermelons in the spring garden. Some means of warming up the soil and protecting from late frosts is needed with these crops.

One commercial solution to this problem is the *hotcap*, a waxpaper tent that sets down over the plants and acts like a greenhouse. Using hotcaps it is easy to get two weeks ahead of your neighbor. Cucumbers, etc. can be seeded directly under the hotcap, or started even earlier in pots indoors and transplanted out under the hotcap later, just as you would do with tomatoes. Hotcap techniques also protect tender seedlings from cutworms.

Homemade hotcaps include: coffee cans with the bottom cut out, using the plastic lid for a top on cold days and nights; milk cartons with the bottom cut in flap fashion; or plastic milk bottles with the bottom cut out and the lid left off.

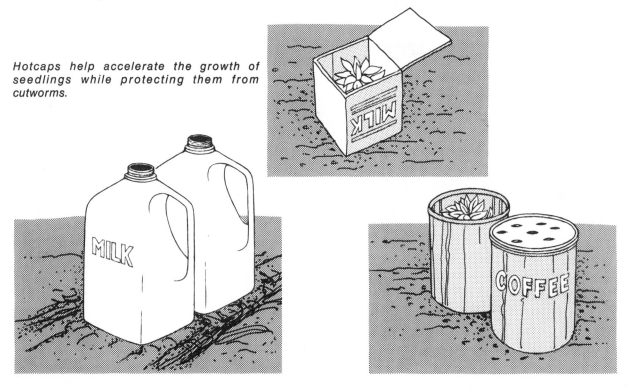

Hotcaps help accelerate the growth of seedlings while protecting them from cutworms.

seed sources

Burgess Seed & Plant Co. Box 2000, Galesburg, Mich. 49053. Beautiful catalog with a few unusual varieties worth trying in the South.

W. Atlee Burpee Co., Clinton, Iowa 52732. A must for anyone that orders seeds. Many varieties are available that are recommended for the South.

William Dam Seeds, Highway #8, West Flamboro, Ontario, Canada. Canada may not seem like a very likely place to order seeds for a southern garden, but some of the cool season vegetable varieties may have promise. Many unusual varieties are offered.

D.V. Burrell Seed Co., Box 150, Rocky Ford, Colo. 81067. Many standard varieties, with special emphasis on melons. Also a good selection of peppers.

Henry Field Seed and Nursery Co., 407 Sycamore St., Shenandoah, Iowa 51601. Has several hard to find vegetable varieties.

Glecklers Seedmen Metamora, Ohio 43540. Nothing fancy, just a price list and brief description it is often the sole source of a number of unusual varieties.

Joseph Harris Co., Moreton Farm, Rochester, N.Y. 14624. Many good varieties for the southern gardener.

H.G. Hastings Co., Box 4088, Atlanta, Georgia 30302. Many southern varieties, but not a complete source.

Kilgore's Seed Co., 1400 West First Street, Sanford, Florida 32771. Good source for southern varieties.

Nichols Garden Nursery, 1190 North Pacific Highway, Albany, Oregon 97321. A great source for unusual varieties of vegetables and herbs.

Geo. W. Park Seed Co. Greenwood South Carolina. 29646. A beautiful catalog. Great to curl up with on a cold night and dream of gardens to come.

Porter & Son, Seedsmen, Stephenville, Texas 76401. No color pictures but many recommended varieties at reasonable prices.

Redwood City Seed Co., P.O. Box 361, Redwood City, California 94064. Source for many oriental varieties.

Reuter Seed Co., 320 N. Carrollton Ave., New Orleans, Louisiana 70119. Many standard southern varieties and several unusual ones.

Seedway Inc., Hall, New York 14463. Standard varieties as well as new introductions.

Otis S. Twilley Seed Co. Salisbury, Maryland, 21801. One of the first to have new state agricultural college varieties as well as standard varieties.

Willhite Melon Seed Farms, Box 85, Weatherford, Texas 76086. The specialty is melons obviously but most other vegetables are available.

(Right) The best place to get most of your seed is from local nurserymen. Sometimes, however, all the varieties you want are not available.

(Left) For those hard-to-find varieties, ordering from a seed catalog is not only a good answer, but it's fun just to browse through on a cold winter's day.

GROW YOUR OWN TRANSPLANTS

Your own vegetable transplants are easy to start. Why bother to grow your own? One of the best reasons is that ready-grown transplants of recommended varieties aren't always available. Also, it is just plain fun to grow your own.

First, select seed of varieties recommended by your State Agricultural Extension Service, or varieties that have proven themselves in your garden. Remember, the seed must be sown 6-8 weeks prior to transplanting.

Materials You Will Need

Once you have the right seed, all the supplies you'll need for growing transplants are:

    a sharp pencil
    vermiculite
    styrofoam hot cups
    plastic bags
    potting soil
    a tray that will hold water
    a watering can
    a soluble fertilizer
    a sunny window,
    wide-spectrum fluorescent lights or
    a coldframe or greenhouse

Begin by writing the variety name on the side of a cup. Punch four holes in the side of the cup at the bottom. Fill the cup ⅔ full with potting soil and add a ¼-inch layer of vermiculite on top. Next, sow 25-30 seeds per cup and cover them with a ¼-inch layer of vermiculite.

Starting the Seedlings

Set the cups in a tray of water and let them soak until the water becomes visible at the top of the vermiculite; then set aside to drain. You may have to weight down the cups if they try to float.

After the water drains, put the cup in a plastic bag; seal the bag with a twist tie, and place in a warm spot out of direct sunlight. As soon as seedlings emerge (one to two weeks) you may remove the cup from the bag, but be sure to keep the seedlings watered.

Styrofoam cups make excellent growing containers for transplants.

When the first set of true leaves develops you're ready to transplant each seedling to an individual pot (styrofoam cup, peat pot, etc.). Again, poke holes in the cups which will receive the transplants, write the variety on each, then fill them with a damp potting soil (buy a sterilized soil mix or use the one suggested under "Potting Mixture, page 21.)

If the soil is moist enough, a pencil pushed into the soil with a twisting motion will leave a clean planting hole as it is removed. Fill all the transplanting pots and make all the holes prior to transplanting the first seedling. This way you lessen the chance of tender roots drying out while you get ready.

Transplanting Procedures

When all is ready for the transplant be sure to water the seedlings, since this permits easy removal from the pot with less chance of damage. Carefully knock out the soil containing the seedlings by tapping the cup on the edge of a table, then carefully break the soil ball apart to disengage and untangle the seedlings.

As you transfer the seedlings handle them by the leaves only; if you damage the stems the plants will die or be stunted. If the roots are too long to fit into the planting hole, it doesn't hurt to pinch a portion off. Be sure to avoid cramming the roots into the hole in a jammed-up position.

When closing the hole, firm the soil against the roots with a lever-like action of the pencil. Insert the pencil into the soil next to the seedling, and pull toward it, thus closing the hole. This helps to avoid air pockets that may be left around the roots, and it also avoids damage to the stem if fingers were used in a pinching manner to close the hole.

Water the seedling carefully with the hose at a trickle, or use a small watering can. If the plant is washed over into the soil, pick it up—it will have a better chance of survival if it is standing upright. Place the plants where they will receive sun all day or until about 3:00 P.M.

Coldframes and Hotframes

Putting the plants where they will get a full day of sun is easy in the summer. In fact, you may want to provide afternoon shade during this season; but growing transplants during the winter for spring planting is another problem. A sunny window will support a few plants, but chances are they will still be a little weak and spindly from lack of light. The new "wide-spectrum" fluorescent lights are better, but buying these will increase the cost of your transplants. If you have a greenhouse you have it made, but most gardeners have neither a greenhouse nor the extra money to spend on one. In this case the best answer is a coldframe or hotframe.

A coldframe is usually adequate in most areas of the South, but a hotframe with a heating cable imbedded 4-6 inches under the seabed can be used.

(Text continued on page 35)

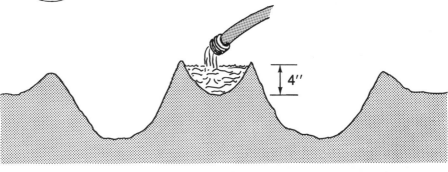

Special germination technique for fall vegetables: 1) Open a furrow 4 inches deep on top of a planting ridge; fill with water and allow it to soak in; 2) Sow seed on top of moist soil; 3) Cover soil with ¼ inch of fine mulch such as sawdust or pine bark; 4) Cover seed with soil no more than 3 times its average thickness.

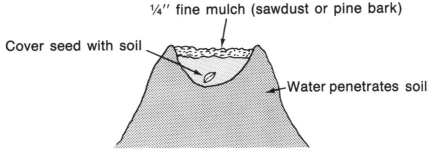

¼" fine mulch (sawdust or pine bark)

Cover seed with soil

Water penetrates soil

Vegetable transplants 33

building an electric hotbed

Picking A Location. Select an area for your hotbed that has good natural drainage so there's little chance of water standing in the bed. It's best to situate the hotbed near an electical outlet and a water tap. Make sure that buildings, trees, etc. do not block sunlight from the bed. Preferably it should be located with a southern exposure so it receives maximum sunlight. Some form of windbreak on the north side will help. This is why many hotbeds are located on the south side of a building.

What Size To Build. You can have an electric hotbed that's almost any size, but the standard 6' x 3' is sufficient for most gardeners.

Heating Cables. Electric heating cables are available, either with lead or plastic covering, and both give good results. The most important consideration is to select a cable with an adequate number of watts per square foot of bed area. Ten watts per square foot is usually adequate in the South. You'll also need a thermostat, but one is included with most cables. The thermostat should have an operating temperature range from approximately 30-120°F, and it should be one that can be partially buried in the soil. Place the thermostat ⅓ of the way across the width of the bed and about the same distance from the end wall. Set it where it is partially buried in the soil; this way it is affected by both soil and air temperatures. Do not place the thermostat directly above a heating cable or allow it to come in contact with one of the cables.

Covering Materials. Many gardeners use a glass covering for hotbeds, but fiberglass is also good. Polyethylene plastic can be used if there is enough slope to prevent water from collecting in the plastic.

Construction Materials. Most hotbeds are constructed out of wood, although some prefabricated kits made from aluminum may be available. Wood should be at least 2 inches thick, and it's also important to provide weather stripping at joints with the cover. Wood should be treated with copper napthenate to retard decay. Do not use wood-treating materials such as creosote or pentaclorophenol.

Hotbeds can also be constructed from masonry blocks, but the open joints with this construction material permit air leakage and may decrease heat efficiency.

Ground Preparation. To ensure good drainage dig the bed area out to a depth of 8 inches, then, after the walls have been constructed, tamp gravel to a depth of 6 inches into the excavated space. This gravel layer will ensure proper drainage. Cover gravel with burlap or wire screening to prevent sand from sifting down into the gravel layer. Approximately 2 inches of sand is needed on top of the gravel layer to protect the heating cable from damage.

Construction. The back wall of the hotbed should be 18 inches above the level where the heating cable is placed. Sidewalls are sloped approximately 1 inch per foot of width. For example, if the bed is 6 feet wide the front wall will be 12 inches high, while the back wall is 18 inches high. Six inches of soil in the hotbed provides 6 inches of space along the front edge, and this is generally plenty for the plants. If the bed was excavated extend the walls to the bottom of this area. If it was not excavated extend the walls 4 inches below the level at which the heating cable is placed. Hinge the back of the sash so that it can be raised up and propped open with a board to allow access to the plants and ventilation. Soil is usually banked against the outside of the walls to serve as further insulation and prevent air leakage.

(Continued)

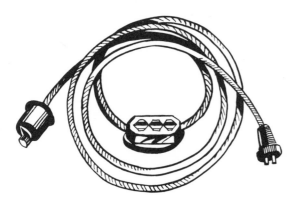

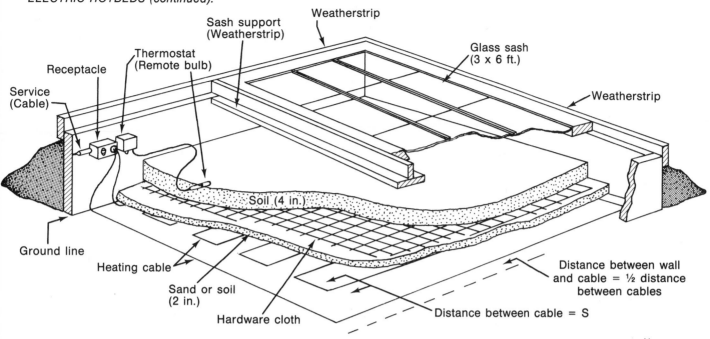

Service (Cable)
Receptacle
Thermostat (Remote bulb)
Sash support (Weatherstrip)
Weatherstrip
Glass sash (3 x 6 ft.)
Weatherstrip
Soil (4 in.)
Ground line
Heating cable
Sand or soil (2 in.)
Hardware cloth
Distance between wall and cable = ½ distance between cables
Distance between cable = S

Installing The Heating Cable. Lay the cable either on soil at the bottom of the bed or, if the bed was excavated, on the sand covering the gravel. Try to space the cable as uniformly as possible. Once the cable is in position cover it with 2 inches of loose soil or sand and place ½-inch mesh hardware cloth on top of this layer. This will prevent damage to the cable when digging in the bed.

Never cross one cable over another or try to shorten the length of the cable, as this may cause the cable to burn out.

Wiring. Proper wiring is very important. A weather-proof service switch that has been properly fused and grounded should be installed by a licensed electrician. Make sure that all connections to the heating cable are watertight. Large beds will probably require a 3-wire, 230-volt line.

Using The Hotbed. You'll need 4 to 6 inches of soil in the bed, or you can grow plants in individual pots. Be sure to use prepared potting soil that's free of insects, disease and weed seeds. A soil temperature of 70 to 75° is ideal for most plants, and you'll find that germination is rapid with a heating cable. Cool season crops such as cabbage and lettuce will require slightly lower tempera-

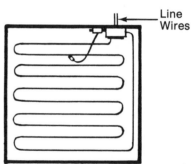

Line Wires

tures than will warm season crops like peppers and tomatoes.

Check both soil and air temperature with thermometers. In the South, even during the winter, it's quite possible for air temperatures to get greater than 85°, so you'll need to open the hotbed for ventilation in the winter as well as in the summer.

When you're producing transplants in late summer for fall planting it will probably be necessary to keep the coldframe open all the time, perhaps substituting a shading material for the clear cover to protect the plants from sunscald in late afternoon.

COLDFRAMES (continued).

A coldframe can be built from lumber (preferably 2 inches thick), concrete boxes, brick, concrete, etc., and it can be almost any size. A 30-inch by 36-inch coldframe will hold plenty of plants. The back

of the frame needs to be higher (24 inch) than the front (12 inch) to allow for rapid drainage off of the frame cover. Glass or fiberglass (clear only, not green tinted) is adequate for a covering. Don't use polyethylene plastic unless the cover has considerable slope because water collects during heavy rains and causes it to sag.

It's best to dig out about 1 foot of soil beneath the frame and replace this with a bottom layer of fresh manure 8 inches thick covered with a 4-inch layer of sand or soil mix. Use soil mix if you plan to grow transplants directly in the soil rather than in individual pots. A layer of manure provides sufficient heat in most areas of the South. Soil should be mounded up around the outside of the frame to give additional insulation. Be sure to raise the cover for ventilation on sunny days, however, as temperatures can become rather extreme. About 2 weeks prior to transplanting begin to harden the plants off so they will be better able to survive outside conditions. This "hardening off" is accomplished by allowing the plants to dry out more (even wilting slightly), by withholding fertilizer, and by allowing temperatures to stay cooler. To keep temperatures cool leave the cover partially up on all but the coldest nights.

Summer transplants grown for fall planting won't need a coldframe nor will they need any hardening off, since frosts are not a concern at transplanting time and you'll want to get them going as quickly as possible so they'll produce before the first frost in the fall.

If you have a greenhouse, try to keep daytime temperatures between 70 and 80°F, with nighttime temperatures 10 to 15° lower. Fluorescent light should be placed 6 to 12 inches above seedling flats for a duration of 12 to 16 hours per day.

Continuing Care of Seedlings

After the first week, use a liquid fertilizer in the watering can to promote stronger, more vigorous plants. To prevent insect and disease injury, spray with diazinon or malathion, and maneb weekly. In six to eight weeks the plants should be ready for the garden.

To grow just a few plants, try planting two or three seeds in the center of each cup as previously suggested, and cut out two of the seedlings after they begin to develop their first set of true leaves. This technique saves the extra transplanting stage, so it's worth the disadvantage of producing a fewer number of seedlings per package of seed. For the homeowner there's usually too much seed in a package anyway.

WATERING

Even in the usually rainy South, watering is required during the growing season in most years. Here's a recommendation by the California Agricultural Extension Service that will be helpful

Sun and/or prevailing wind

Wood shingles will provide protection for newly set transplants.

in determining watering frequency when rain is lacking.

If your soil is	When to water
Clay	Every 8-12 days in hot weather Every 15-18 days in cool weather
Sand	Every 4-6 days in hot weather Every 7-9 days in cool weather
Loam	Every 7-8 days in hot weather Every 10-15 days in cool weather

Don't ignore your plants. If they show signs of wilting they probably need water. Try pushing a steel rod in the soil to check the depth of moist soil.

When you do water, water early and thoroughly. Try to shut down sprinkler type irrigation equipment by 2:00 p.m. and apply 1½ to 2 inches of water. A few coffee cans set around the garden make good rain gauges. If you do this, foliage will be dry by evening and there will be less chance of disease. Timing is not as critical with flood (furrow) irrigation or drip irrigation.

Drip Irrigation

Drip Irrigation makes even watering easy. It also conserves water, reduces the potential for accumulation of salts, lessens the chance of spreading diseases in splashing water, and is less

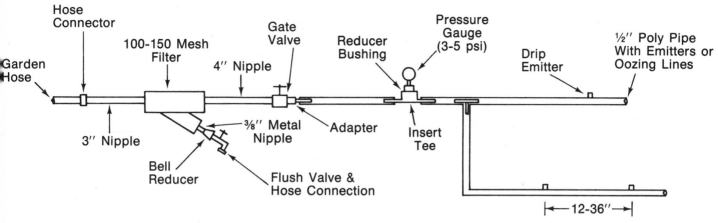

Drip irrigation system for a small garden. Redrawn from Roland E. Roberts, "Mini-Gardening with Drip Irrigation," The Texas Horticulturist, *Vol. 1, No. 1, Spring, 1974.*

likely to damage soil structure or cause erosion. This system of watering applies small, frequent amounts of water. A number of drip irrigation systems have been developed in the last few years. Some use emitters which allow a slow drip of water to soak into the soil at intervals along lines of ½-inch diameter plastic pipe; others involve a porous line which oozes moisture all along its length. Both types can be set up to operate automatically or with a minimum of manual effort. If mulching is employed with these types of irrigation systems, weeds are at most a minor problem.

A basic home garden drip irrigation system might be set up as indicated in the diagram.

Each system varies a bit, but technical data on how much water is being delivered at a specific pressure will probably come with the equipment. If not, prop a couple of emitters over cans and measure the amount accumulated after an hour. Determine the average flow per emitter and multiply by the number of emitters.

The following table and formula make it easy to determine how much water is needed to apply 1-4 acre inches of water. Once this figure is determined for a particular amount of water, say 1 inch, just divide by the amount of water delivered by your drip irrigation system per hour and you'll know approximately how many hours to water.

Conversion of Water Volume in Acre Inches to Gallons Per Acre, Gallons Per 1000 Square Feet, and Gallons for Smaller Areas

Acre inches	Gallons per acre	Gallons per 1000 sq ft	Gallons per 100 sq ft	Gallons for your garden (sq ft)
1	27,154	623	62.3	_____
2	54,308	1250	125	_____
3	81,462	1873	187	_____
4	108,616	2500	250	_____

An example using a figure from the table in a simple formula to show how to determine the approximate amount of water to apply to a mini garden to get the equivalent of an acre inch of irrigation:

$$\frac{\text{Number of square feet in garden}}{100} \times 62.3 = \begin{array}{l}\text{Gallons to apply to your} \\ \text{garden to get an acre inch} \\ \text{of water.}\end{array}$$

Table and diagram reprinted with permission of Dr. R.E. Roberts, Extension Vegetable Specialist, Texas Agricultural Extension Service from "Mini-Gardening with Drip Irrigation," *The Texas Horticulturist*, Vol. 1, No. 1, p. 12.

MULCHING

Mulching is the answer to all your home garden weed problems. Hoeing is hard work, and even though you keep your hoe sharp (it's about as much work filing a hoe as it is hoeing) or use one of the new fangled "scuffle hoes," this type of work makes gardening a little less fun. If you plan to hand pick the weeds plant a little garden.

Weed-control chemicals sound great at first, but their use is complicated in the home garden where many different crops are planted together. There is no herbicide that can be used on all vegetable crops, and some of these chemicals last too long or they may wash into other parts of the garden.

There are a number of materials that can be used as a mulch: pine bark, bagasse (sugar cane pulp), sawdust, and bark chips work well, but two of the most readily available and cheap materials are newspaper and hay. Almost everyone accumulates newspapers, and hay that has been spoiled by rain can be purchased for next to nothing.

How do newspapers and hay combine to keep weeds out of the garden? Easy. First, soak a quantity of the newspapers in water for several hours or

# of hydroponics
and greenhouse tomatoes

"Grow thousands of delicious tomatoes hydroponically in the controlled environment of a greenhouse." Sounds great, doesn't it? Unfortunately, this statement overlooks many of the limitations of hyproponic, soil-less culture, and greenhouse vegetable production.

Hydroponic Culture Problems. Soil-less culture requires a very accurate and constant monitoring of the nutrient solution. Soil reaction (pH) and the availability of elements necessary for plant growth can change rapidly. The gravel, or whatever material is used to support the plant roots in hydroponic culture, doesn't have the buffering capacity of soil. A growing media such as a mixture of pine bark, vermiculite, and fertilizer elements would be more properly termed a synthetic soil—technically not a hydroponic media. The latter type of mix responds much like soil even though it may not contain any. Where you have good soil or a good soil substitute, why make something complicated, more complicated.

Hydroponic systems are also much more expensive to install than ground bed systems. In a study conducted by Norman Brints, Extension Area Economist-Management, Texas A&M University, the total investment in soil bed, tomato greenhouse operations ranged from $1.31 to $2.30 per square foot in the Gulf Coast area. A hydroponics operation can easily cost four to five times as much to set up.

Greenhouse Tomato Problems. Growing greenhouse tomatoes is no way to retire unless you're looking forward to working harder in retirement than you did for the first 20 to 40 years of employment. Greenhouse tomato growing is an intensive, exact and demanding business which requires a thorough knowledge of horticulture, pathology, and entomology.

1) One of the major complaints from former greenhouse tomato growers in the South has been poor fruit set during the winter due to low light conditions. Tomatoes only shed pollen on bright sunny days and haze, smog, and clouds reduce this pollination significantly along the Gulf Coast.

2) Pest control problems are another major complaint of southern gardeners. Insect pests, such as white flies, tomato pin worms, red spider mites, and leaf miners, develop in large numbers and are difficult to control in our southern climate. Diseases are also a problem. Gray leaf mold and tobacco mosaic virus are especially troublesome and are not related to the type of growing media. Nematodes, soil-born microscopic worms which attack the roots, are another serious pest.

3) The often-seen claim of year-round production in the controlled environment of a greenhouse is misleading. Even with the best cooling and shading, little production can be anticipated in the summer (when temperatures are greater than 90°F). Combine this with lower prices due to the competition of field grown tomatoes and increased pest control problems, and the economics of greenhouse tomato production becomes less attractive.

What about the homeowner that just wants to grow a few greenhouse vegetables in the winter? That's fine, but if you decide to grow them hydroponically you're taking on additional burdens. One of the first problems often encountered is finding the chemicals suggested in hydroponic nutrient formulas. Regular fertilizers won't work. With hydroponics you'll probably end up learning more about chemistry than growing vegetables.

MULCHING (continued).
overnight. This will keep them from blowing all over the neighborhood while you're trying to put them down in the garden. Spread the wet newspapers six to eight sheets thick over the garden area. For row crops, leave just enough space to plant a row of seed. With transplanted crops, cover the whole area and cut out holes to set the plants in. Then spread a six to eight-inch layer of old hay over the paper. By the time weeds grow through this mulch, your crops will be up and producing. Sprinkling a little fertilizer over the mulch through the growing season will help supply enough nitrogen to break down the newspaper so you can dig it in as an additional source of organic matter for the soil.

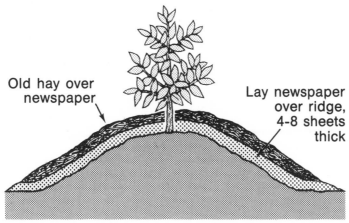

Old hay over newspaper

Lay newspaper over ridge, 4-8 sheets thick

Newspaper and hay may be used as an effective mulch.

Another Way

Some gardeners like to use newspapers in old plastic clothes bags like you get from the cleaners. They just slip the bags over an 8-sheet section (or more) of newspaper and lay this combination down on the rows. The most efficient way to do this is to prepare the beds and leave a trench along each side. Lay the paper plus plastic across the row and overlap each section a couple of inches. With an ice pick, poke holes in both sides of this lap and use an old piece of coat hanger bent in a U shape and pushed through these holes into the ground to hold the sections together. Do this on both sides and you won't have to worry about the mulch blowing away. This system works best with transplanted crops like tomatoes. Under the mulch, lay a length of soaker hose or one of the new drip irrigation systems, and you've got it made.

Black Plastic and Special Paper Mulches. Rolls of black plastic can be used as suggested for the paper and plastic, just cut holes where the plants need to go. Recently, however, the cost of black plastic has gone up quite a bit. Because black absorbs heat it gets too hot for summer use, but spraying with a thin white latex paint will solve this problem.

Another material which is even better is a special paper mulch. Unlike the black plastic, this material will not allow nutgrass to penetrate, except where it is torn. As yet it is relatively unavailable. Other paper mulches are available, including some in light colors for use in the late summer when absorption of heat by the dark colors is undesirable. Some gardeners use brown kraft paper covered with an organic mulch.

Hoeing is hard work and it takes some of the fun out of gardening, but a little bit is necessary even if you have a good mulch.

bees

As a rule, gardeners are interested in other areas of the biological sciences. They may raise rabbits, chickens, ducks, earthworms, or something very logical, like bees. There is an unjustified fear of bees among those who are not familiar with these wonderous little creatures. Although some people are seriously allergic to bee stings, this reaction is very rare, and if you fear death from a bee sting contact your family physician or an allergy specialist and have him prescribe an Emergency Insect Sting Kit. If you work with your bees carefully and wear protective clothing, you should rarely, if ever, get stung.

Regardless of whether you decide to become a beekeeper or not there's a good chance you'll have an opportunity to decide the fate of a swarm of bees at some time or another. Bees swarm quite commonly during the spring gardening season and to the uninitiated a boiling swarm of bees can be frightening. Bees that have swarmed are usually quite docile, however, unless they have been disturbed by flying rocks or other thoughtless actions. Rather than exterminate these swarms, turn them over to one of the local Beekeepers Associations. They'll have someone come by to get them. Don't expect them to be overjoyed to get a swarm in the walls of your house. This is a special problem and most beekeepers won't fool with it. If they do, it certainly won't be for free.

Bees are gardener's natural friends. Many of our favorite fruits and vegetables depend on bees for good pollination. These include: beans, cucumber, muskmelons, peppers, pumpkins, squash, sunflowers, watermelons, blackberries, blueberries, grapes, peaches, pears, persimmons, plums, and strawberries. Bees also pollinate many other plants that don't grow well here or that are grown for seed in other areas of the United States. Strangely enough, most of the honeyflow comes from insignificant flowers of trees, shrubs, and weeds. One of the most important of these in the deep South is the Chinese Tallow Tree *(Sapium sebiferum)*. It yields a light, good quality honey.

If you have an interest in gardening you'll find bees a complementary hobby. For more information contact one of the local bee associations in your area and attend one of their meetings.

Books on beekeeping are a logical place to start, and most seasoned beekeepers recommend you start with a beginner's manual first. A good beginner's book is *First Lessons in Beekeeping.* Several magazines are also available, including *Gleanings in Bee Culture,* Medina, Ohio 44256 and *The American Bee Journal,* Hamilton, Illinois 62341.

Not only will your garden do better with bees around, but chances are you'll be able to harvest delicious, healthful honey that will make you do better, too.

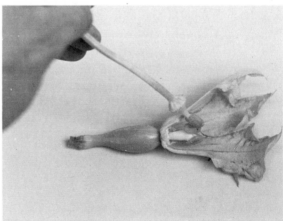

One way to pollinate squash without bees is to take the male blooms, tear off the petals, and dab some of the pollen onto the female blooms. This should be done in the morning while the blooms are open and receptive.

sprouts

A simple sprout chamber can be constructed with a quart jar, scrap lumber, and a cardboard box.

If it rains the first weekend you had planned to work in the garden, or if it's just too hot, try another type of gardening indoors that is not dependent on the weather—growing sprouts. This is an excellent project for children because you get results in three or four days rather than in months. Sprouts are not only fun and easy to grow, they are very nutritious. In the germination process a great many vitamins, enzymes and other food materials are made more readily available. For example, the Vitamin C content of soybean sprouts from the time that they first sprout until after 72 hours increases 700 percent.

Most types of seeds can be sprouted; just be careful to avoid plants known to be poisonous, such as tomatoes and other toxic members of the plant family. Some of the more common seeds used for sprouting are: mung beans, soybeans, lentils, alfalfa, chickpeas, sesame, oats, wheat, rye, sunflower, pumpkin, fenugreek, radish, black mustard, red clover, corn, flax, garden peas, safflower, turnip, barley, and southern peas (blackeye's, etc.). Some are easier, particularly

mung beans and alfalfa seeds, which are also two of the best.

Sprouting seeds is simple. You can use almost anything, from a covered crock to special seed sprouting devices. The following is an easy-to-construct seed sprouter. It makes a great family project as well as a good project for 4-H clubs and Boy or Girl Scout groups. You'll need the following materials: a quart-size jar for large sprouts or a pint-size jar for small ones, a medium-size cardboard box (approximately 6 inches by 12 inches should be adequate), a piece of quarter-inch plywood, two small pieces of two-by-four-inch wood, a piece of cheesecloth, and seeds for sprouting. You will also need some tools—a small-bladed saw to cut a hole in the plywood for the jar to rest in, a drill to start the hole so that you can cut an oval piece out of the center of the plywood, and, if you want to add an extra touch to your sprouting chamber, some paint.

(Continued on next page)

Construct the chamber by either removing the top or bottom of the box (if flaps have been pulled open, cut these off and consider this the bottom). Cut through three sides of the top of the box to make a lid for the sprouting chamber, then measure a piece of plywood to fit snugly inside the box. Use two pieces of two-by-four to make a stand for this plywood and cut an oval hole slightly larger than the jar so the jar can be set at a slant on the rack.

Soak small seeds for 6 to 8 hours and larger ones for 12 to 15 hours. Most sprouters recommend drinking the fluid the seeds have been soaked in or pouring it on your plants. Two to three tablespoons of small seeds such as alfalfa are usually adequate, while about ¼ cup of the larger seeds (makes 2 cups of sprouts) will usually be sufficient. Put seeds in the sprouter and invert the sprouter in the sprouting chamber with the cheesecloth, secured by a rubber band, dangling in a pan of water underneath the rack. This keeps the cheesecloth covering the jar constantly moist, thus preventing the sprouts from drying out. Once or twice a day take the sprouting chamber out and rinse the seeds, then put them back in the chamber. Be sure to check the pan for water, as it evaporates readily.

Most sprouts will be ready in two to three days. Some, such as alfalfa sprouts, will be even more nutritious if exposed to light for 12 hours or so. Be sure to use fresh seeds designed for sprouting and put your sprouting chamber in an area where temperatures are approximately 70 to 85°.

Most seeds can be sprouted using two bowls. Soak the seeds as usual, drain them and put them in one of the bowls. Cover the seeds with several thickness of paper towel. Then invert the second bowl over the first. It helps if the second bowl is slightly smaller. You can use ceramic bowls but plastic ones work even better because they usually fit together tighter. The plastic bowls with special snap on lids should be good to use also. Be sure to rinse the seeds several times a day just as with the other technique. In 3 to 4 days you'll have a bowl full of sprouts.

You should find this new type of gardening an excellent variation, not only to your outdoor garden efforts, but also to your dietary habits. There's nothing more tasty and nutritious than a peanut butter and beansprout sandwich or a garden salad topped with a generous amount of alfalfa sprouts.

Controlling Those Pests

Once your vegetable garden is up and growing, lookout! The bugs and diseases won't be far behind. Pest control, especially in the vegetable garden, is more complicated than it once was because of concern about persistent pesticides. Many of the old stand-bys like DDT and lindane are now prohibited in the vegetable garden because they simply last too long. In many cases these persistent chlorinated hydrocarbons were less toxic than some of the alternative chemicals we use today.

Why do we have to worry about bugs and diseases? The same mild climate that allows us to grow some vegetables year-round also allows many pest to overwinter, pests that might otherwise die in a long, cold winter.

There's little reason to expect that Nature will control all these pests in an ecologically sound way. When we plant a garden we change alot of Nature's ideas on ecology. For instance, a single species of plant doesn't grow naturally in a row. Planting many of one species (monoculture) leads to an accumulation of those pests that attack the plant.

Crop rotation would seem to be the answer to pest build-up problems, but rotation is difficult in the small home garden. Many of our favorite vegetables are closely related; tomatoes, eggplants, and peppers for instance. As you might expect, some of the same diseases and insects attack all three. In addition, some pests can remain viable for several years. As an example, Southern Blight forms a resting structure called a sclerotia that may remain alive and capable of infection for up to 3 or 4 years in the soil. This organism can also exist almost indefinitely on dead organic matter as a saphrophyte. As if this weren't enough, Southern Blight attacks a wide range of host plants.

Most garden vegetables have been changed considerably from their original wild form. In fact, many of the ancestors of our modern vegetables can no longer be found. We've developed them primarily for flavor and texture. Disease and insect resistance is important, but no one wants to eat disease-resistant lettuce if it tastes as bitter as quinine and has the texture of leather.

We're so used to good quality fruits and vegetables that it's difficult to accept lettuce with holes in the leaves or apples with worms in the fruit. Pesticides have done an admirable job of controlling most pests, most of the time. If you decide to use few or no pesticides, quality will likely suffer.

Use as many cultural control methods and nontoxic controls as possible. Not everything in the garden needs to be sprayed each time you spray, nor can the same spray be used for all plants and all pests. The following recommendations are nontoxic and will help to shift Nature in your favor.

NATURAL DISEASE AND PEST CONTROLS

● Disease control can be improved by spacing plants adequately and planting on hills to allow better air circulation. This is particularly helpful in controlling squash fruit rot—a black whiskery growth followed by decay of the fruit. You can reduce the severity of this disease by immediately removing any diseased fruit and mulching the plants to prevent splashing the soil when watering or during rainy periods.

● Hand picking certain insect pests can be very helpful, particularly if you start early in the season. Tomato hornworms, squash bugs, and stink bugs (wear gloves, they're appropriately named) can be effectively controlled in small areas by daily dunkings in a can of diesel or by applying sufficient pressure to the pest with the sole of your shoe. Boards laid around the garden will attract a number of small garden pests, and daily (in the morning) lifting and stomping will help.

● Mulching with aluminum foil will repel aphids.

● High-pressure streams of water are effective in reducing numbers of small insects like aphids (plant lice) and mites. Just give the plants a good washing down, being certain to direct the spray to the underside of the leaves as well as to the top.

● Insects have diseases just like people do. One of these, *Bacillus thuringiensis*, can effectively control cabbage loopers, tomato hornworms, and the larvae of the IO moth (a big, green, stinging caterpillar). They eat the bacterium, become ill and stop feeding almost immediately, then die. Try to spray this material in the evening or early morning because it is broken down by ultra-violet light. Best of all, this preparation is nontoxic to other animals. Other relatively nontoxic pesticides are: rotenone, pyrethrum and ryania.

● Cutworms can easily be prevented from cutting off tomato transplants by wrapping the stem with a cardboard collar or by placing cans or milk cartons with both ends removed around the plants.

● Keep debris and plant refuse cleaned out of the garden to reduce disease and insect build-up.

● Plant resistant varieties where possible. For instance, tomatoes resistant to root-knot nematodes are: Better Boy, Pelican, and Improved Summertime.

● Healthy plants growing in a rich, organic soil are less susceptible to many pests. Put an extra ounce of effort into soil preparation, plant at the right time, and reap a bountiful harvest.

Dusting can be a very efficient means of controlling insect and disease pests. This duster is especially good because the dust nozzle is on the side of the tube. This allows easy application of the dust material to the underside as well as to the top of the foliage.

CHEMICAL PESTICIDES

Nontoxic pest controls should certainly be used in the home garden when possible, but what about those frustrating pests like leaf miner and leaf-spotting fungal diseases? Especially where you are concerned with quality, the use of chemical pesticides is almost essential.

Unfortunately, no single chemical or combination of chemicals controls *all* garden pests. But you can use a minimum of chemicals to control most pests. Special chemicals are needed only when a particular problem arises.

Insecticides

Some chemical insecticides readily available for use in the home garden are:

● Malathion. The common misconception is that this chemical is extremely dangerous, like

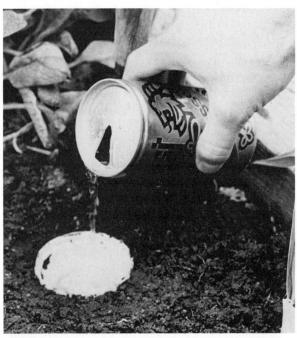

Beer is a good slug, snail, and pill bug attractant. By embedding small containers, such as the covers from spray cans, in the soil and filling them with beer, you can attract and drown many of these pests without the danger of using chemical pesticides. One problem: it makes the beer unfit to drink.

another organophosphate, parathion. The latter is not available for general use, however. Organophosphates are not long-lasting and for this reason their use is becoming more widespread. Malathion is a good general-purpose insecticide for controlling aphids, mites, and a number of chewing insects. It has one fault—it is unstable in alkaline water. This sometimes makes malathion less effective than it should be. Unfortunately, spray buffers are not yet available in small quantities for the home gardener.

• Diazinon. Often recommended as the one and only insecticide needed, it is quite versatile. It is generally not as effective against caterpillars as sevin (carbaryl) or *Bacillus thuringiensis* (the latter is good for control of certain larvae only).

• Sevin (Carbaryl). This is a good, relatively safe material to use. It is generally effective against chewing insects, but it may be devastating to many beneficial predatory insects and to bees. One homeowner made the remark that he thought Sevin came with spider mite eggs in the box. This isn't true, but by killing good guys like lady beetles the other resistant pests have an easy time building up in large populations.

• Kelthane. Kelthane is a miticide that may become a necessary chemical in your spray arsenal. Red spider mites suck juices out of the plant, and although small, they build up in large populations and can do tremendous damage. Small webs may be evident, and a yellow, stippled appearance is often characteristic of leaves infested with spider mites. Spraying at three-day intervals, first with diazinon or malathion followed by kelthane, and then with the diazinon again will usually do the job. Wettable sulfur, a less toxic chemical, is also effective on mites, and it has fungicidal properties as well. Don't use it on members of the cucurbit family (squash, cucumbers, pumpkins, etc.) or in hot weather (temperature greater than 85°F).

There are certainly other insecticides that can be used in the garden, and those mentioned here can't be used on everything—READ THE LABEL BEFORE APPLYING ANYTHING.

Fungicides

Diseases are also a problem in our humid climate. Some of the better fungicides for home garden use are:

• Maneb (or maneb + a zinc ion) is a relatively nontoxic, good general-purpose fungicide. It requires a fairly long waiting period between spray application and harvest (five to seven days de-

pending on the crop). Maneb is compatible with most insecticides and can be used in mixing a combination spray. Zineb is similar and is used for many of the same garden diseases.

• Captan is another general-purpose fungicide that is particularly useful in home orchard sprays as well as in the garden. Captan is also effective in the control of seedling diseases such as damping off. It, too, is compatible with most insecticides.

• Terraclor (PCNB) is used to combat soil-born diseases such as damping off and Southern blight. It is not generally used for foliar diseases.

• Chlorothalonil (Broad Spectrum Fungicide, Bravo) is especially useful because it requires a comparatively short waiting period from spray to harvest and it is relatively nontoxic. This is one of the newer fungicides, and it is very effective.

• Copper fungicides have low toxicities, can be used on many vegetables (as long as temperatures are below 85°F), and do not require a long harvest interval. These materials may not be compatible with all insecticides.

When applying sprays be certain to direct the spray to the underside of the foliage as well as to the top. Wear a long-sleeved shirt and be sure to wash up. Always take a shower after spraying.

A good combination spray that can be used on a wide variety of plants is diazinon or malathion plus chlorothalonil. Be sure to read label directions thoroughly and follow recommendations accurately. Combination sprays should be mixed according to directions for each. As an example, if the insecticide recommendation is one teaspoon per gallon and the fungicide recommendation is one teaspoon per gallon—to prepare one gallon of the combination spray put one teaspoon of each in one gallon of water.

KEEPING VARMINTS OUT OF THE GARDEN

Most home gardeners don't have much trouble with varmints like deer, possums, raccoons, armadillos, gophers, and woodchucks; but if you have a garden that goes unattended for awhile, such as at a vacation home or out on the farm somewhere, you'll probably have trouble with varmints getting in and helping you harvest the vegetables or destroying young plants. Some of the varmints you can anticipate having trouble with and ways to keep them out of your garden are:

Deer—One of the most effective means of keeping deer out of your garden is to string cotton balls soaked in lion's scent (lion urine from the zoo) around the garden. Also, strange as it may seem, manure from wild animals such as cats, bears and other ferocious beasts reportedly keeps deer out of the garden. Bloodmeal has been reported to keep them out, but most gardeners have had no success with this. A six-foot woven wire fence with two strands of barbed wire above will keep deer out, but this is rather expensive. Pop bottles stuck in the ground which catch the wind and produce a whistling sound are sometimes reported to keep deer out of the garden.

Raccoons—Again, the wild animal manure may help, as may bloodmeal, but raccoons are difficult to keep out of the garden. They climb well and may get in.

Rabbits—Keep rabbits out with a fence that's at least a couple of feet high, and bury the fence a foot or so in the soil.

Armadillos—Armadillos are extremely difficult to keep out of the garden because they burrow well, so they may even get under a shallow or partially buried fence. It may be necessary to stay up a few nights and physically destroy the animals. Wild animal manure may also discourage them. By erecting a fence at least 30 to 36 inches high, with a concrete footing extending 18 to 24 inches into the soil and a close union between fence and footing, you should be able to keep armadillos out. A large dog penned up inside the garden will scare them off, but the dog may trample all of your garden vegetables. Soil insects are one of the main food sources for armadillos. Treating the soil with an insecticide such as diazinon will eliminate grubs and other armadillo food sources and may help discourage this pest.

Moles, gophers, etc.—Poison baits put into the runs of these animals will help eliminate them. Barriers such as recommended for armadillos and rabbits also help.

Birds—To prevent bird damage you will almost have to plant extra seed or cover the area with a plastic netting. Noise-making devices will keep them away for a short period, and you may find that little strips of tin foil, pie pans, or colored bits of cloth will also scare off birds temporarily, but they'll eventually figure it out and come back. One method recommended for keeping birds away from the vegetables is to put rubber snakes in the garden. Apparently, birds don't like snakes. Try oil pieces of rubber hose cut up and hung around in the trees and on stakes throughout the garden. You can try a scarecrow if you wish, but chances are it won't keep the birds out very long, though it will add a rustic charm to your garden.

Miscellaneous Techniques. Several other methods have been described as effective in keeping out varmints. One involves leaving a transitor radio out in the garden under a protective cover and tuned to an all-night radio station. The varmints think there's a party going on and avoid the garden patch.

Another recommendation is to sprinkle black pepper out in the corn field about the time the corn is ripening. This reportedly keeps raccoons from getting into it.

One final technique to try is an electric fence. For small varmints, it will need to be 6 inches or closer to the ground, while to keep cattle out it will need to be set at 18-24 inches.

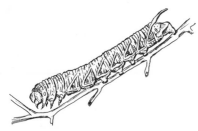

Tomato Hornworm
This big green worm devastates tomato plants. If you find it before it does much damage, hand picking is an excellent control. Otherwise, spray with carbaryl or Bacillus thuringiensis.

Colorado Potato Beetle
Can do rapid damage to garden plants. Control with carbaryl or malathion.

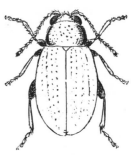

Flea Beetle
The appearance of many small holes on the foliage of peppers, beans, potatoes and other garden vegetables is an indication that the small flea beetles are at work. Carbaryl and malathion are controls.

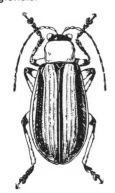

Striped Cucumber Beetle
These pests feed on roots as larvae and as adults. In addition, they carry bacterial and viral diseases. Control with carbaryl or malathion.

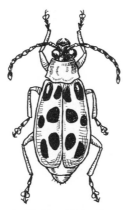

Spotted Cucumber Beetle
These pests, like the striped cucumber beetles, feed on roots as larvae and as adults. In addition, they carry bacterial and viral diseases. Control with carbaryl or malathion.

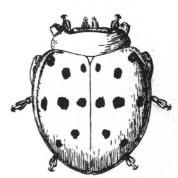

Mexican Bean Beetle
Can do rapid damage to garden plants. Control with carbaryl or malathion.

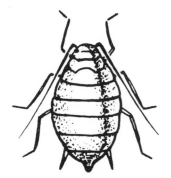

Aphid (Plant Louse)
These small, pear-shaped, sucking insects are usually found on young, growing shoots. In addition to reducing plant vigor by feeding on the sap, they also transmit disease. Control with malathion or nicotine sulfate.

Leaf-Footed Bug
This pest commonly attacks okra and tomatoes in the South. It is a sucking insect and does damage similar to that done by the stink bug. Control with diazinon or malathion where these chemicals are registered for use. A very limited number of pesticides are registered for use on okra, however.

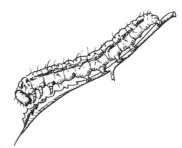

Corn Earworm
The roasting ears in the grocery store don't have the ends cut off to make them line up in neat rows. They are cut off primarily to remove corn earworms. This difficult pest can be controlled by planting varieties resistant to attack, such as Aristogold Hybrid, and by dusting the silks with 10% carbaryl every 3 days until they turn brown.

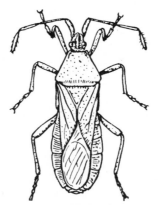

Cabbage Looper

This little green inchworm was almost impossible to control in the home garden except by physically smashing them. Today, the bacterial spray containing the organism Bacillus thuringiensis *is an effective control.*

Squash Bug

Squash bugs in the nymphal stage are relatively easy to control with carbaryl or endosulfan. Once they become adults, however, physical removal of the insect and eggs left on the underside of the leaves will be necessary.

Spider Mite

This garden pest is one of the most difficult to control. When infestations are severe it is best to pull up the plants and start over. Where applicable, sulfur is an excellent control as is dicofol (kelthane). Malathion and diazinon will also give some control.

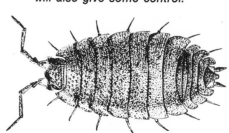

Slugs, Snails and Pill Bugs

Beware of using slug and snail baits in the garden that are not allowed for use around vegetable crops. In recent years improper use of these materials has often necessitated destroying the garden. Carbaryl will give some control, and beer used as a bait is also somewhat effective. If you decide to use beer, dig a hole and place shallow receptacles, such as the tops from aerosol spray cans, level with the soil and partially fill with beer. You'll soon have a spray cap full of slugs, snails and pill bugs, and beer that is no longer fit to drink. Dusting plants lightly with wood ashes is another old remedy.

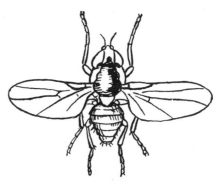

Sharpshooter

This small, sucking insect is particularly fond of okra and can be seen quickly scurrying to the opposite side of okra stems whenever approached. Fortunately it seems to do little damage. Because of the limited registration of pesticides for use on okra, and the minimum amount of damage done, its control is usually unnecessary.

Leaf Miner

White, squiggly lines on the leaves of tomatoes, beans, cucumbers, and other garden vegetables are indications of leaf miner damage. Leaf miners are any of several gnat-sized flies whose larvae tunnel between leaf cell layers. Regular and early sprayings of diazinon or malathion in a weekly spray program will provide control.

What to Grow

It's standard to suggest that you choose vegetables you like to eat, but don't be afraid to experiment. Your garden should consist of at least 75 percent standard varieties recommended by your state Extension Service, but try a few new varieties and new vegetables.

Should the garden be planted with the new hybrids only? Not necessarily. Most are great. The new hybrids usually have better vigor and are more disease-resistant. They may produce earlier and they often have better flavor; but sometimes they have a shorter harvest interval, especially since so many varieties have been developed for mechanical harvesting, where the whole crop must be picked at once. This is sometimes desirable in the home garden, though. For instance, when you want to put up pickles but only have a small space. If you plant a variety that sets its crop all at one time you'll have a concentrated harvest to make pickles with, otherwise, you'll get a few cucumbers every day and have trouble getting enough fresh ones at one time.

Can you save your own seed? Definitely not with hybrids. The seedlings revert back to less desirable forms. Hybrid seed is produced by crossing two in-bred lines which, hopefully, combine to produce vigorous offspring with the best characteristics of both parents. The parents of hybrid seed are less than spectacular, and the seedlings from hybrid plants are usually even less impressive. If you save the seed of some standard varieties it should be from isolated plants or those that are not usually cross-pollinated. Tomatoes and beans are rarely cross-pollinated, but cucumbers, squash, all members of the cabbage and mustard families, and okra are readily cross-pollinated.

When saving seed (either your own or last year's seed packs), make sure it is dry. Laying the seed out for a week on paper towels in a dry location in the house will usually suffice. Then try to fill air-tight containers as full as possible (this excludes oxygen and reduces respiration) and put the container in the refrigerator.

Different seeds last different lengths of time. Short-lived seeds (1 to 2 years) include: corn, onions, parsley, parsnip, and salsify. Moderately long-lived seeds (3 to 5 years) include: asparagus, bean, brussels sprouts, cabbage, carrot, cauliflower, celery, kale, lettuce, okra, peas, pepper, radish, spinach, turnip, and watermelon. Long-lived seeds (more than 5 years) include: beet, cucumber, eggplant, muskmelon, and tomato.

Some Planting Hints for the Southern Gardener

Beware of varieties with names like 'Summer Bibb'—not that they can't be grown here, but they usually won't do well in the summer. The variety name 'Summer Bibb' is describing a summer in Vermont, not in Houston or Atlanta. Many varieties recommended for the North don't do well in the South. Excellent examples of this are the large-fruited tomato varieties, Ponderosa and Beefsteak. These may do well in mild summer areas of Pennsylvania, but in the South they are a waste of time when compared to better-adapted varieties recommended by southern Agriculture Universities.

Don't expect some vegetables, regardless of variety, to perform as well in the South as they do in the North. Most of the vegetables which require a long, mild growing season, such as English peas, Brussels sprouts, and rutabagas, get caught by temperature extremes—either too hot or too cold—when grown in the South. If there is one vegetable we *can't* grow, it is probably rhubarb.

Another difficult vegetable is asparagus. In this case, it is not a matter of the weather being too hot or too cold, but a lack of extended dormancy that causes problems. Because asparagus tries to grow most of the year in the South, it fails to store the food reserves which promote prolific growth of large, thick spears over a long period in the spring.

Onion varieties recommended for the North are generally unsatisfactory in the South because they require long days to initiate bulbs. Many areas of the South do not get much more than 14 hours of daylight on the longest day of the year. A variety requiring 14½ to 15 hours to initiate bulbs just is not going to work in the South. If it does get a long enough day, it may come when temperatures are too warm for a good bulbing response. Unfortunately, many of the sets and transplants offered southern gardeners are of the northern types. Varieties recommended for the South include Grano, Granex, Excel, and Bermuda.

PLANTING CHART

Vegetables	Depth of Plant or Seed Planting in Inches	Inches of Distance Between — Rows	Inches of Distance Between — Plants	Spring Planting in Regard to Average Frost-Free Date	Fall Planting in Regard to Average Fall-Freeze-Date	No. Days Ready for Use	Average Length of Harvest Season Days	Average Crop Expected per 100 feet	Approx. Planting per Person — Fresh	Approx. Planting per Person — (Storage) Canning or Freezing
Asparagus	6-8, 1-1½	36-48	18	4 to 6 wks. before	not recommended	730	60	30 lb.	10-15 pl.	10-15 pl.
Beans, snap bush	1-1½	24-36	3-4	on to 8 wks. after	8 to 10 wks. before	45-60	14	120 lb.	15-16 ft.	15-20 ft.
Beans, snap pole	1-1½	36-48	4-6	on to 4 wks. after	14 to 16 wks. before	60-70	30	150 lb.	5-6 ft.	8-10 ft.
Beans, Lima bush	1-1½	30-36	3-4	on to 4 wks. after	8 to 10 wks. before	65-80	14	25 lb. shelled	10-15 ft.	15-20 ft.
Beans, Lima pole	1-1½	36-48	12-18	on to 4 wks. after	14 to 16 wks. before	75-85	40	50 lb. shelled	5-6 ft.	8-10 ft.
Beets	1	14-24	2	4 to 6 wks. before	8 to 16 wks. before	50-60	30	150 lb.	5-10 ft.	10-20 ft.
Broccoli	½	24-36	14-24	4 to 6 wks. before	10 to 16 wks. before	60-80	40	100 lb.	3-5 pl.	5-6 pl.
Brussels Sprouts	½	24-36	14-24	4 to 6 wks. before	10 to 14 wks. before	90-100	21	75 lb.	2-5 pl.	5-8 pl.
Cabbage	½	24-36	14-24	4 to 6 wks. before	10 to 16 wks. before	60-90	40	150 lb.	3-4 pl.	5-10 pl.
Cabbage, Chinese	½	18-30	8-12	4 to 6 wks. before	12 to 14 wks. before	65-70	21	80 heads	3-10 ft.	—
Carrot	½	14-24	2	4 to 6 wks. before	12 to 14 wks. before	70-80	21	100 lb.	5-10 ft.	10-15 ft.
Cauliflower	½	24-36	14-24	not recommended	10 to 16 wks. before	70-90	14	100 lb.	3-5 pl.	8-12 pl.
Chard, Swiss	1	18-30	6	2 to 6 wks. before	12 to 16 wks. before	45-55	40	75 lb.	3-5 pl.	8-12 pl.
Collard (Kale)	½	18-36	8-16	2 to 6 wks. before	8 to 12 wks. before	50-80	60	100 lb.	5-10 ft.	5-10 ft.
Corn, sweet	1-2	24-36	12-18	on to 6 wks. after	12 to 14 wks. before	70-90	10	10 doz.	10-15 ft.	30-50 ft.
Cucumber	½	48-72	24-48	on to 6 wks. after	10 to 12 wks. before	50-70	30	120 lb.	1-2 hls.	3-5 hls.
Eggplant	½	24-36	18-24	2 to 6 wks. after	12 to 16 wks. before	80-90	90	100 lb.	2-3 pl.	2-3 pl.
Garlic	1-2	14-24	2-4	not recommended	4 to 6 wks. before	140-150	—	40 lb.	—	1-5 ft.
Kohlrabi	½	14-24	4-6	2 to 6 wks. before	12 to 16 wks. before	55-75	14	75 lb.	3-5 ft.	5-10 ft.
Lettuce	½	14-24	2-3	6 wks. before-2 wks. after	10 to 14 wks. before	40-80	21	50 lb.	5-15 ft.	—
Muskmelon (Cantaloupe)	1	60-96	24-36	2 to 8 wks. after	14 to 16 wks. before	85-100	30	100 frts.	3-5 hls.	—
Mustard	½	14-24	6-12	on to 6 wks. after	10 to 16 wks. before	30-40	30	100 lb.	5-10 ft.	10-15 ft.
Okra	1	36-42	24	2 to 12 wks. after	12 to 16 wks. before	55-65	90	100 lb.	4-6 ft.	6-10 ft.
Onion (plants)	1-2	14-24	2-3	4 to 10 wks. before	not recommended	80-120	40	100 lb.	3-5 ft.	30-50 ft.
Onion (seed)	½	14-24	2-3	6 to 8 wks. before	8 to 10 wks. before	90-120	40	100 lb.	3-5 ft.	30-50 ft.
Parsley	⅛	14-24	2-4	on to 6 wks. before	6 to 16 wks. before	70-90	90	30 lb.	1-3 ft.	1-3 ft.
Peas, English	2-3	18-36	1	2 to 8 wks. before	2 to 12 wks. before	55-90	7	20 lb.	15-20 ft.	40-60 ft.
Peas, Southern	2-3	24-36	4-6	2 to 10 wks. after	10 to 12 wks. before	60-70	30	40 lb.	10-15 ft.	20-50 ft.
Pepper	½	24-36	18-24	1 to 8 wks. after	12 to 16 wks. before	60-90	90	60 lb.	3-5 pl.	3-5 pl.
Potato, Irish	4	30-36	10-15	4 to 6 wks. before	14 to 16 wks. before	75-100	—	100 lb.	50-100 ft.	—
Potato, sweet	3-5	36-48	12-16	2 to 6 wks. after	not recommended	100-130	—	100 lb.	5-10 pl.	10-20 pl.
Pumpkin	1-2	60-96	36-48	1 to 4 wks. after	12 to 14 wks. before	75-100	—	100 lb.	1-2 hls.	1-2 hls.
Radish	½	14-24	1	6 wks. before-4 wks. after	on to 8 wks. before	25-40	7	100 bunches	3-5 ft.	—
Spinach	½	14-24	3-4	1 to 8 wks. before	2 to 16 wks. before	40-60	40	3 bu.	5-10 ft.	10-15 ft.
Squash, summer	1-2	36-60	18-36	1 to 4 wks. after	12 to 15 wks. before	50-60	40	150 lb.	2-3 hls.	2-3 hls.
Squash, winter	1-2	60-96	24-48	1 to 4 wks. after	12 to 14 wks. before	85-100	—	100 lb.	1-3 hls.	1-3 hls.
Tomato	4-6, ½	24-48	18-36	on to 8 wks. after	12 to 14 wks. before	70-90	40	100 lb.	3-5 pl.	5-10 pl.
Turnip, greens	½	14-24	2-3	2 to 6 wks. before	2 to 12 wks. before	30	40	50-100 lb.	5-10 ft.	—
Turnip, roots	½	14-24	2-3	2 to 6 wks. before	2 to 12 wks. before	30-60	30	50-100 lb.	5-10 ft.	5-10 ft.
Watermelon	1-2	72-96	36-72	2 to 8 wks. after	14 to 16 wks. before	80-100	30	40 frts.	2-4 hls.	—

Adapted from *A Planning Guide for Your Home Garden*, Texas Agricultural Extension Service, Texas A&M University System.

Cool Season Vegetables

Beets

other roots in the row to attain a maximum diameter of 2 to 3 inches. If thinning is necessary prior to the 1-inch stage the entire plant is often cooked. Roots that grow over 2 to 3 inches in diameter are rather tough and unpalatable.

Diseases. Beet diseases are a minor concern in the home garden. There are a few leaf-spotting diseases which won't even require control, and a couple of viruses which cannot be controlled—fortunately, these aren't much of a problem either.

Insects. Leaf miners sometimes cause a small amount of damage to beets, but they, too, are nothing to be concerned about in the home garden.

Another Problem. Beets sometimes get internal black spots which result from a boron deficiency. These hard or corky black spots are scattered through the root. The problem commonly occurs with tight soils having a high pH, or light, overused sandy soils. Borax, just like you buy from the grocery store, can be used at the rate of 4 oz. per 1,000 square feet. Mix the borax with water and apply to the soil surface.

History. The beet originated in Europe, where it was developed as a root vegetable. Beets were probably used first as a green leafy vegetable. Swiss Chard is today's improved form of this leafy beet. In the U.S. beets were first mentioned as a root vegetable in the nineteenth century.

Culture. Beets, like most root vegetables, require a loose soil that is high in phosphorous and potassium. They also like a neutral to slightly alkaline soil (pH 7.0-7.5). Acid soils must be limed for beet crops. Beets should be thinned to stand 2-3 inches apart in the row, with rows 14-24 inches apart.

Recommended Varieties: Detroit Dark Red, Green Top Bunching, Asgrow Wonder, and Early Wonder. For fun, try white beets, yellow beets or the long cylindrical varieties.

Harvesting. Begin harvesting beets when they are about 1 inch in diameter. By doing this you allow

Broccoli

History. Broccoli is a member of the cabbage, or cole, family. The term "sprouting" broccoli has recently been contracted to just broccoli. Broccoli became widely popular around 1940, so it is a relatively new vegetable.

Culture. Broccoli is easy to grow in the home garden. It requires cool weather, and although transplants may be started in late summer, they do not begin active growth until temperatures cool down. Broccoli can be grown both as a fall crop and again as an early spring crop. Space plants 14-24 inches apart in the row, with rows 24-36 inches apart.

Recommended varieties: The new hybrid varieties are definitely worth planting. The Green Comet hybrid is a particularly good variety.

Harvesting. Broccoli should be harvested while the flower buds are still tight. Depending on the variety, the central flower bud may be 3 to 6 inches in diameter. Smaller side shoots can also be harvested after this central head is cut, and they too should be picked while the flower buds are still tight. Six to eight inches of the stem can also be harvested as long as the stem is tender.

Diseases. Broccoli and cabbage suffer from many of the same diseases, but perhaps not to the same degree. Of major concern are downey mildew and wire stem disease. The latter is a phase of damping-off that stunts the growth of the plant and causes the stems to be small, tough, and woody. Fungicide applications are usually not necessary, but a general purpose fungicide may be used.

Insects. By far, the pest most injurious to all members of the cabbage family is the cabbage looper, a small green inch-worm. This pest has become resistant to many insecticides. Fortunately, the new biological sprays, bacterial preparations that are nontoxic to humans, make controlling this pest much less difficult.

Brussel sprouts

History. Brussels sprouts, another member of the cabbage family, originated in Europe. The crop derives its name from the fact that it has been

grown in the vicinity of Brussels, Belgium for hundreds of years. It is considered a minor crop in the South, but it can be grown with some success if planted in the fall.

Culture. Space Brussels sprouts 14-24 inches in the row, with rows 24-36 inches apart. Plant in the fall in a very fertile soil. Pinch out the terminal bud and/or remove the lower leaves as the sprouts form in the leaf axils. Pinching the terminal bud stimulates rapid and uniform sprout formation, but it may reduce the total yield.

Recommended Varieties: Jade Cross hybrid.

Harvesting. Brussels sprouts should be snapped or cut off while they are still tight and ¾ to 1½ inches in diameter. If you wait until the lower leaves begin to turn yellow you may be sacrificing quality.

Insects and Diseases. Same as for cabbage.

Cabbage

History. Cabbage grows wild along the seacoast of England and in various locales along the southern coast of Europe. It has been used as a vegetable since 2500 B.C. Many popular cool season vegetables are descendants of cabbage. Broccoli, cauliflower, Brussels sprouts, collards (cabbage may even be a descendant of the collard), kale, and kohlrabi are all classified in the same genus as cabbage.

Culture. Cabbage is not too popular in small- or medium-sized southern vegetable gardens. It is grown commercially throughout the South and is generally available at a good price and in good quality. Nevertheless, if you want to grow cabbage, try one of the Savoy (crinkle-leafed) varieties or red cabbage. Red cabbage is a heavy feeder and needs a loose, well-draining soil. Space plants 14 to 24 inches apart in the row, with rows 24 to 36 inches apart.

Recommended Varieties: These can be generally summed up as early-maturing hybrids—Green Varieties: Market Prize, Gourmet and Greenback; Red Varieties: Red Acre, Meteor; Savoy types: Chieftan Savoy.

Harvesting. Cabbage can be harvested almost anytime, even when no larger than a softball. Too long a delay in harvesting combined with considerable rain late in the season causes some varieties to split.

Diseases. Cabbage diseases are usually a minor problem in the home garden, but there are a number of troublesome organisms, such as Black rot. Black rot is caused by a bacterium that usually infects plants at the leaf margins. Yellow areas develop along the margin, resulting in an inverted V-shape. Veins also become black and are particularly noticeable when held up to the light. The bacterium is seed-born, so obtain disease-free seed. Crop rotation for at least two years is also of value.

Fusarium yellow causes the plant foliage to turn yellowish-green, and plants are wilted and stunted. This disease should not be much of a problem in home gardens, but if it does occur move cole crops (cabbage, broccoli, etc.) to another area of the garden.

Downey mildew disease is noticeable on the underside of leaves as a white downey growth. Removing infected debris after the growing season, rotation, and use of a fungicide are helpful in controlling this disease.

Black leg shows up on leaves and stems as small spots with grayish centers and many black dots in the spots. Eventually the entire root system is destroyed by this rotting organism. The disease (a fungus) is carried in the seed and also persists in plant refuse for several years. Disease-free seed, rotation, and good sanitation all help.

Alternaria leaf spot is caused by a fungus, and it, like many diseases affecting the cabbage family, is carried on the seed. Plant seed which has been hot water-treated. A general-purpose fungicide also helps, but this is usually not necessary.

Wire stem disease is caused by the same organism *(Rhizoctonia)* that causes damping-off, and it is a latter stage of damping off that did not completely kill the plant. The stems of infected plants are smaller, tougher, and have a woody appearance when compared to stems of normal, healthy plants. Crop rotation and avoiding the use of fungus-infected transplants are controls.

Soft rot is a bacterial disease that usually infects commerical crops, developing during storage or in transit. In the home garden the disease can be avoided easily by careful handling of the cabbage when harvesting. Nematodes and southern blight can also be a problem (see page 45).

Mosaic virus may occasionally infect members of the cabbage family, but with the exception of controlling insects that are potential transmitters of the disease, little can be done in the garden to prevent it.

Insects. The cabbage looper is a caterpillar that plagues all members of the cabbage family. It is resistant to most pesticides but can be easily controlled with a biological spray containing a bacterium that sickens and eventually kills the caterpillar. Spray this material late in the evening or in the early morning because it is broken down by ultra-violet light and thus is less effective if applied at mid-day. Aphids are a sporadic problem, but they are easily controlled with chemical pesticides or by simply washing the plants down with a high-pressure spray of water.

Carrots

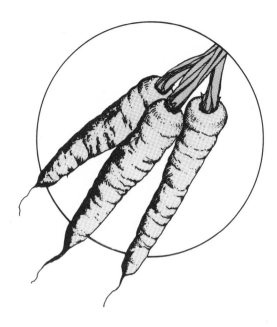

History. The wild carrot originated in Europe, Asia, and, perhaps, other areas of the world. It has not been grown as long as some vegetables, but carrots have been a popular vegetable in Europe at least since the thirteen century, and in America since the arrival of early settlers.

Culture. Carrots are available at relatively low prices and in fairly good quality in produce sections of the supermarket. Thus, their value in the home garden, except to try gourmet or unusual varieties, is doubtful. Plants should be thinned to 2 inches apart in the row, with rows 14 to 24 inches apart. Carrots must have a deep, loose soil to develop properly, unless you grow some of the short, stubby varieties. If planted in tight clay soils they may end up looking like little orange accordions.

Recommended Varieties: Nantes, Danvers, Gold Spike. For fun you might try growing White Belgium carrots, some of the tiny carrots which are reportedly of superior quality, or some of the many other interesting varieties offered in seed catalogs.

Harvesting. Carrots can be harvested at almost any stage until they begin to get tough and woody. The small tender carrots (about finger-size) are usually considered to be of superior quality. Most carrots are harvested when the top of the root is about ¾-inch in diameter.

Diseases. A virus disease may occasionally infect plants, causing the roots to be bitter and distasteful. Controlling the disease-transmitting leaf hopper with a chemical pesticide is the principle prevention.

Insects. Several root-burrowing insects may occasionally damage carrots, but unless they are known to be a pest, soil treatment with an insecticide will probably not be required.

Cauliflower

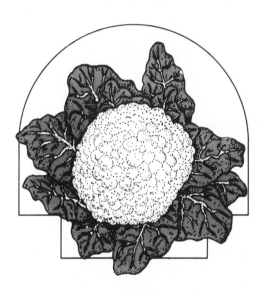

History. Cauliflower is another of the many forms of cabbage that originated in Europe. Cauliflower is not as easily grown as some other members of the cabbage family, but especially good are the quick-maturing varieties when planted in early fall to mature before the first hard frost.

Culture. Growing cauliflower is much the same as growing cabbage and other members of this family, except that as the cauliflower (curd) develops to the size of a small teacup the leaves need to be pulled up around the head and tied loosely to exclude light. This practice, called *blanching,* prevents the head from developing a dingy, spotted appearance. Space plants 14 to 24 inches apart in the row with, rows 24 to 36 inches apart.

Recommended Varieties: The early hybrid varieties, such as Snowball hybrid, are the most satisfactory types for the home garden in the South.

Harvesting. Cauliflower heads are usually harvested when 4 to 8 inches in diameter and before they begin to get discolored.

Diseases and Insects. See cabbage.

Collards

History. The collard, perhaps, is the forerunner of all cabbage varieties. It would seem to be nothing more than a cabbage which doesn't form a head. Because all the leaves are exposed to sunlight, it is even more nutritious than cabbage. It is similar to another vegetable, kale, which is more readily appreciated in the northeastern U.S. Interestingly enough, a frilly-leaved collard (kale) often appears and is rouged out of collard fields in the South.

Culture. Plants should be spaced 8 to 16 inches apart in the row, with rows 18 to 36 inches apart. Both kale and collards are at their best during cooler weather. The flavor is supposedly improved by a frost. Both vegetables will survive the summer and often grow for several years before going to seed. Strange, almost tree-like cabbage plants seen in southern gardens are actually collard greens which have been continuously harvested from the bottom up. It is one of our most productive vegetables, and one that belongs in every southern garden, small or large.

Recommended Varieties: Georgia, Vates, Kale, Dwarf Siberian, and most other varieties.

Harvesting. Typically, collard leaves are harvested beginning with the outer or lower leaves, eventually creating what looks like a small tree. Regardless of where you decide to begin picking, best quality leaves will be 8 to 10 inches long.

Diseases and Insects. See cabbage.

Kohlrabi

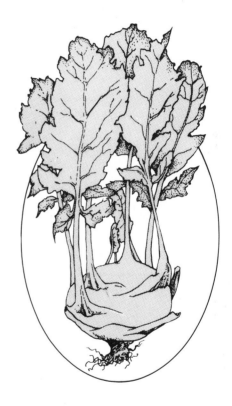

History. Origin similar to other members of the cabbage family.

Culture. Kohlrabi can be cropped almost continuously through the cool weather. Staggered plantings being sown every two weeks. It is a delicious vegetable which tastes very much like a sweet mild turnip. Kohlrabi is also a strange-looking vegetable, and, if nothing else, it should make an interesting conversation piece in the garden.

Plants should be spaced 4 to 6 inches apart in the row, with rows 14 to 24 inches apart. Very few varieties are available. White and Purple Vienna are the only ones offered.

Harvesting. Kohlrabi should be harvested while still 2 to 3 inches in diameter, otherwise it becomes tough and woody.

Insects and Diseases. Same as for cabbage, minimal.

Lettuce

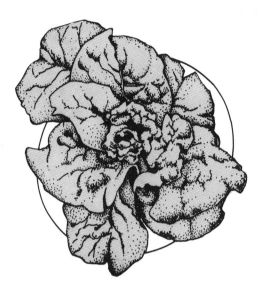

History. Lettuce probably came from Europe and Asia and has been grown for at least 2,500 years. There are at least four types of lettuce popular in the U.S.: the loose leaf type, Romaine, the bibb or butterhead type, and head lettuce.

Culture. Lettuce is strictly a cool season vegetable. Names like Summer Bibb no doubt refer to a summer in Vermont. Most areas of the South produce small or poor quality lettuce during the summer. Lettuce that is not actively growing is often bitter. To produce good, high quality lettuce your soil must be well prepared with lots of organic matter, nitrogen, and water.

A common mistake when planting lettuce is to cover the seed too deeply. Lettuce seed requires light for germination. It should be scattered along the row and lightly raked or scratched into the soil. Be sure to keep it moist until it has germinated and is well-established (about 2 to 3 weeks). Thin lettuce plants to stand 2 to 3 inches apart in the row, with rows 14 to 24 inches apart. Several thinnings may be necessary and plants should eventually stand 6 to 8 inches apart in the row. Lettuce must be thinned if it is to produce. Crowded lettuce plants produce small leaves that are difficult to harvest. Of the four types, head lettuce, the one typically seen wrapped in plastic in the grocery store, is by far the most difficult to grow. Often just about the time it is heading and appears ready to produce beautiful heads a hard freeze damages the entire plant or at least blackens the wrapper leaves.

Recommended Varieties: Several varieties of head lettuce developed for the South are available, two of which are Great Lakes 6238 and Imperial 847. Some good loose leaf types of lettuce are Oak Leaf, Bronze and Ruby (two very ornamental vegetables for the home garden), Salad Bowl, Slo Bolt, Black-Seeded Simpson, and Grand Rapids. Of the Romaine varieties, the best is ValMaine, a downey mildew-resistant variety developed in the South. Of the bibb types, Bibb, Summer Bibb, Buttercrunch and Deer Tongue are very reliable in southern gardens.

Harvesting. In the home garden, lettuce, particularly the leafy types, can be harvested over a long period of time simply by removing the outer leaves. Romaine or Bibb varieties will probably require harvesting the entire plant at one time.

Diseases. There are several diseases which attack lettuce, but in the home garden most are not very important. Damping-off organisms that affect young seedlings are the most bothersome. These organisms can be avoided somewhat by planting in well-drained soils and using a fungicide-treated seed.

Insects. Cutworms can be a problem with lettuce in the home garden, especially young seedlings. Control cutworms with insecticides if damage is severe. Cabbage loopers may also cause trouble, and the new biological sprays (bacterial preparations) provide effective control of this pest. Aphids (plant lice) sometimes damage lettuce and are readily controlled with insecticides. Leaf hoppers are a problem because they transmit certain virus diseases, but they do not pose much of a threat in the home garden.

Mustard greens

History. The mustard greens grown in the South are derived from Asiatic species. In the home gar-

Insects. The same insect pests that attack members of the cabbage family attack mustard greens. Cabbage loopers are probably the worst pest, but they are easily controlled with biological sprays. Aphids, or plant lice, also attack mustard at times. These pests are also controlled with biological sprays, except for certain chewing insects (caterpillars, leaf-eating beetles) that are not susceptible to the biological spray.

The pesticides recommended for these insects require rather long waiting periods. A pesticide that requires waiting two weeks before you can harvest will have dropped to a low enough toxicity rate for the insects to begin feeding again long before the two weeks are up. The total effect may be worse than doing nothing and having to harvest leaves with a few holes in them.

den the curled-leaved varieties and a very mild variety called Spinach Mustard (Tendergreen) are very popular. Commerically, the main varieties grown are the plain-leaved types.

Culture. Mustard requires about the same growing conditions as collard greens. Space plants 6 to 12 inches apart in the row, with rows 14 to 24 inches apart. Mustard, like the collard green, is fairly tolerant of hot weather, and thus can be grown into late spring or even during early summer in the northernmost areas of the South.

Recommended Varieties: Southern Giant Curled, Florida Broad Leaf, and Tendergreen or Spinach Mustard. Many of the exotic oriental varieties of mustard, such as Japanese White Celery Mustard, can be substituted.

Harvesting. Mustard is harvested like collards or other greens—when the leaves are 10 to 15 inches along.

Diseases. The same diseases that affect cabbage and turnips are a problem with mustard. In urban areas sulfur dioxide injury from air pollution is sometimes a problem in the home garden. Obviously, the damage may not be as serious as it would be to the commerical grower. Boron deficiency is another problem. Mustard greens grown in a boron-deficient soil make slow growth and lack the typical rich green color, even if supplied with high amounts of nitrogen. Apply 4 ounces of borax in enough water to cover 1000 square feet when the plants are about one week old.

Onions

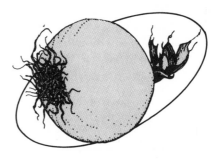

History. The various forms of onions have been eaten for centuries. Many of the nearly 500 species have been used to develop the numerous varieties, which may be divided into several types of onions: the standard bulbing onion, the bunching or multiplying onion, the shallot, the leek, garlic, and, of course, chives.

Culture. All onions require about the same growing conditions. Basically, a very rich, loose, fertile soil. If your soil is tight and/or poorly drained you'll need to construct a raised bed. At least 2 inches of organic matter, such as rotted manure, and 4-5 pounds of a fertilizer, such as 8-24-24 per 100 square feet, will usually be adequate to get onions off to a good start. As growth begins in early spring you will want to sidedress with nitrogen when the leaves are in the 4-5 leaf stage. This usually occurs shortly after you have transplanted the small plants and they have been established (2-3 weeks). Sidedress with 1 pound of ammonium sulfate (21-0-0) per 100 feet of row or use ¾ pound of ammonium nitrate for the same area. In addition, nitrogen sidedressing will be needed at the same rate every 3 weeks to prevent plants from becoming yellowish and slow-growing.

Bulbing Onions

Onions are a major crop in the South, but many home gardeners don't raise them successfully. Often, it is because they select the wrong varieties, especially with the bulbing type onions. To successfully grow bulbing onions in the South it's necessary to plant short-day varieties. Onions respond both to the length of day and to temperature. Many onion plants and onion sets available in garden centers, feed stores, etc. are long-day onions and are better adapted to northern growing conditions unless they're being grown for green onion use only. Some bulbing onion varieties that respond to short days are: Bermuda, 'Early Grano,' 'Texas Grano 502,' 'Excel,' 'Granex,' 'White Granex,' and 'Eclipse.' Short-day onions that produce red bulbs include 'Tropicana,' and 'Burgundy.' If northern varieties such as 'White Portugal' or 'Sweet Spanish' are used the days don't get long enough (14-16 hours) to stimulate a good bulbing response, or the response comes so late that temperatures are too hot for good production.

Because plants or sets of these bulbing types are not readily available during the January planting season, it's best to start these plants from seed in September, October or November. Seed can be sown rather thickly on a prepared bed, and the onions will grow quite well while young even though crowded. Be sure not to plant the seed deeply. Sprinkle seed over the surface of the soil and lightly rake it in. Since onion seed does not last long in storage, don't hesitate to plant all of the seed. It probably won't be good next year, so don't save it. As the plants reach pencil thickness in January they can then be thinned out and transplanted to other areas in rows 14-24 inches apart, with plants 2-3 inches apart in the row. Transplants much larger or smaller than pencil thickness should be discarded or used for green onions. The large plants are especially prone to bolting or going to seed after exposure to prolonged cold temperatures.

Green Onions

Green onions, also called bunching, multiplying or Welch onions, are well adapted to southern growing conditions. They should be planted in the

fall, usually from seed. Most of the harvestable onions will be produced in late winter and early spring, though with good care they may extend into the summer. Two common varieties available are Evergreen Bunching and Beltsville Bunching.

Shallots

The shallot is another onion of the multiplying type which eventually produces a small bulb. It is popular in the South; in fact, about 90% of the shallots produced in the U.S. are grown in Louisiana. This state has produced several varieties of shallots through the Agricultural Experiment Station at Louisiana State University. Shallots are sometimes used as green onions, and the tops may be chopped up as a substitute for chives. If allowed to mature in late spring, this variety will form bulbs. The shallot often sold in

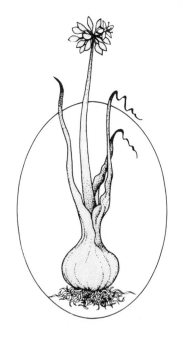

stores as a dry onion, or offered for sale by northern mail order seed and plant companies, is not as well adapted to southern growing conditions as are the Louisiana varieties. Louisiana varieties include Louisiana Evergreen and Delta Giant.

Garlic

Garlic, a member of the onion family, is grown during the same season that onions are, and thus should be planted in the fall or in the winter to mature in the spring. There are a number of varieties, including one called Elephant Garlic which is much larger and apparently milder, and some very small varieties that are extremely pungent, such as recambole. Chives also belong to the onion family and are discussed under "Herbs."

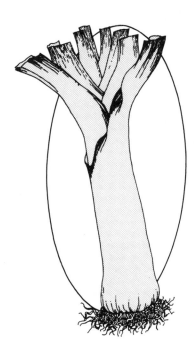

Leeks

Leeks require a long growing season (140 days from seed). They should be planted in trenches 4-6 inches deep in the fall (September-October), and as they begin to enlarge pull up the soil around them to blanch the stems. The most common variety is 'Large American Flag.'

Harvesting. Onions should be harvested anytime they are needed. If planted too thickly the bulbing onions can be used as green onions during the thinning process. Bulbs 2 to 4 inches in diameter are usually left to lay in the garden or preferably in a dry, shaded location for 3 to 4 days. Outdoor storage in most areas of the South is impractical, especially with the poor storage qualities of short-day varieties usually grown. They may be stored for some time in the house in mesh bags. Some people chop up the onions and freeze them for use in cooking. In the South onions hung by the stems in a garage usually rot.

Diseases. Onions' major disease in the home garden is pink root. Although this desease usually doesn't kill the plant, it stunts the bulbs. Once the organism is in the soil, it is difficult to eradicate. It usually comes in on diseased transplants or sets. If the plants have fresh feeder roots check to see if they are pink. This is a good reason to grow your own transplants from seed. Pink root is especially bad on wet, sandy soils.

Resistant varieties are usually marked P.R.R. Some resistant varieties include: 'Texas Early Grano 502 P.R.R.,' 'Excel,' Evergreen Bunching, Beltsville Bunching and the Evergreen Shallot.

Another disease problem is storage rot. Onions are very difficult to store in most of the humid South. If onions are to be used for cooking try chopping them up and freezing them in small plastic freezer bags.

Insects. Thrips are onions' principal insect. They are tiny, rasping insects that cause the leaves to develop brown, elongated spots due to their feeding activity. This is usually the reason onions appear to go down or fade out in the spring. Thrips are relatively easy to control with insecticides. Because recommendations for the use of chemicals may change, they are not included here. The latest recommendations for chemical control of insects and diseases may be obtained from your local county office of the Agricultural Extension Service. Proper protection and controls will help provide healthy, good-sized mature onions.

English peas

History. The English pea has been around for a long time. It was grown by the Romans and Greeks, perhaps having originated in Egypt. There is some confusion about its origin because little distinction was made in the writings of the time between a number of leguminous crops. It is very probable, though, that the English pea, or garden pea, originated in Europe and Western Asia.

Culture. English peas are very difficult to raise in the South, especially in the lower South. When planting in the fall they often begin to bloom just about the time we have a hard frost, and thus the frost-sensitive blooms and small developing pods, are damaged. The plants, however, are quite tolerant of frost. On the other hand, production is severely reduced if English peas are planted in late winter (January through March) because by the time the plants reach flowering and fruiting size, temperatures have become too warm. Fresh, sweet garden peas eaten raw out of the garden are certainly worth the effort though. Particularly worthwhile are the edible-podded or snow pea varieties because there is less waste in shelling the peas. English peas require a relatively fertile, loose, well prepared organic soil that is neither extremely acid (below a pH of 6) nor extremely alkaline (pH greater than 7.5). Plants should be spaced 1 to 2 inches in the row with rows 18 to 36 inches apart. However, spacing depends on the ultimate size of the varieties you plant.

Recommended Varieties: The dwarf, early-maturing varieties are better adapted to the South. Varieties most often recommended for the South include: regular types—Little Marvel, Laxton, Alaska, Cleo, Wando and Premium Gem; Snow pea types—Dwarf Gray Sugar.

With all legumes, the production potential is increased by inoculating seed with nitrogen-fixing bacteria. This is a good practice when legumes are grown in new areas that may be deficient in nitrogen. These inoculants can be purchased from many mail order sources. If seeds are treated with chemicals to retard the development of disease much of the potency of the inoculant may be lost.

Harvesting. The peas should be well filled and the pods should be changing color from dark to light green. Perhaps the best indicator is taste sampling. Pick snow peas while still small and before the seed begins to develop, otherwise the pods will develop fiber and become unpalatable when eaten whole. If snow pea pods should get this large the peas can still be shelled out and used much like English peas.

Diseases. Root rots and several wilting diseases attack English peas. Treated seed may be necessary where this occurs. The main problem with English peas in the South is their poor adaptability to our growing conditions.

Insects. Aphids, or plant lice, are the major insect pest of the English pea in home gardens. They can be easily controlled with insecticide sprays.

Irish potatoes

History. The so-called Irish potato could not be more inappropriately named. Though widely grown and utilized in Ireland, it is nevertheless a native of South America. It was introduced into Europe during the sixteenth century but was not cultivated extensively until the late seventeenth century. In the U.S. it was being cultivated in the early 18th century. Ireland's potato famines in the mid-nineteenth century were caused by a fungus disease, late blight, which resulted in a total loss of the potato crop. The potato as a food source is almost as important today as it was then. Fortunately, resistant varieties and disease-control techniques have been developed, making a serious blight such as this almost impossible today.

Culture. The potato develops best (or at least the tubers do) in cool soil. In the South this necessitates early planting for spring crops or late summer planting for a fall crop. Potatoes are not, however, very tolerant of frost, and the tops are often damaged by a late or early freeze, depending on the season. Even with this minor climatic problem, potatoes can be grown successfully in the South.

Irish potatoes must be grown in a loose, well-draining, acid soil. They generally don't grow well in clay soils. Fortunately, sandy soils are often acid, and all that is needed is to avoid an application of lime. It is said that Irish potatoes are not well-adapted to the small garden. By growing these potatoes in a mulch or compost material above the soil, even a small planting can be productive. This also makes it possible to grow potatoes where clay soil is a problem.

Seed potatoes are readily available in the spring when needed for planting in southern gardens, but finding the right size seed potato for fall planting is usually difficult. In the spring the seed pieces of the seed potatoes are simply cut up into pieces weighing 2 to 3 ounces, perferably with 2 to 3 eyes in each piece. These may be dusted with a fungicide and planted out in the garden row about 4 inches deep, with plants 10 to 15 inches apart in rows 30 to 36 inches apart.

If you grow potatoes above ground in a mulch, plant them very shallow in the soil (1 to 2 inches deep) or in a dished out area on top of the soil. Then place 4 to 6 inches of compost or well-rotted manure and straw over the pieces. This may be followed with another 6 inches or more of compost or straw. Potatoes will grow up through the mulch, forming tubers, and in 4 to 6 weeks you can begin carefully checking into this loose material for new potatoes. These "new potatoes" can then be robbed for 4 to 6 weeks before the potato plant begins to yellow and die down, at which time the whole plant can be dug up and the large tubers harvested. The red varieties seem to grow best using this technique, and they are most often used for "new potatoes." In the late summer or early fall it's important to plant whole seed potatoes. They do not have to be large, quarter to half dollar-size is sufficient, but they do need to be seed potatoes and this is where problem of availability becomes apparent. Even in the spring varieties are sometimes not labeled and you may only know that you are getting red or white certified seed potatoes.

In either spring or fall, do not plant potato tubers from the grocery store. They may have been treated with a sprouting inhibitor and will be reluctant to germinate if they come up at all. Should they come up, they will probably be stunted, often appearing virus-infected. Potatoes purchased from the store, if freshly dug, may need a dormant or rest period and will be slow to grow if, again, they grow at all. There is also a greater potential for getting diseased tubers. Some potato diseases, particularly viruses, do not show symptoms in the tuber and, of course, there's even less chance of getting the recommended varieties. Saving small potatoes from your spring garden is one way to be ready for fall.

Recommended Varieties: White potatoes, Kennebec, red, Red Lasoda, Russett, Norgold.

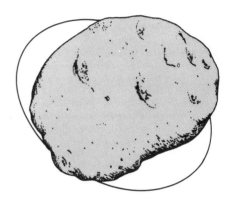

Harvesting. Most of the mature potatoes will be ready for harvest when the plants begin yellowing and drying. However, if potatoes are grown in raised beds in a loose, heavily mulched soil, it is often possible to harvest a few new potatoes long before this time. Just be careful not to damage the plant any more than necessary, and replace the soil or mulch that has been moved away.

Diseases. Potatoes are susceptible to many of the same diseases that attack tomatoes, and a general purpose fungicide will help prevent these if used early in the plants' development and continued on a regular basis. Potatoes also may have disease-like symptoms caused by cultural and/or climatic conditions such as development during warm weather or development with uneven watering. Internal black spot is one such problem, commonly occurring when potatoes mature in a very moist soil.

One of the main problems with potatoes is potato scab, which causes rough, corky areas on the potato. It is best controlled by planting in acid soils with a pH between 4.8 and 5.4. Other diseases are leaf-spotting diseases such as late blight. One of the most prominent, relatively nontoxic materials used to control fungal diseases of potatoes is a copper fungicide known as Bordeaux mixture. Many other diseases can be avoided by planting certified seed potatoes free of the disease.

Insects. The Colorado Potato Beetle is one of the potato's most destructive and widespread insect pests. It is about ⅜ inch long, with black and yellow stripes running longways on the body. It can consume a tremendous leaf area in a short period of time. Early application of insecticide sprays or dust will usually control the pest. Flea beetles are another problem and can be controlled with the same insecticides. Leaf hoppers and aphids, or plant lice, (sucking insects) can also be controlled with insecticides.

Radishes

History. The radish probably came from Europe or Asia. It has been grown for many centuries and was used by the early Egyptians as well as the Greeks.

Culture. Many people have trouble growing radishes successfully, ending up with fairly nice foliage production but very small radishes. Radishes need a loose soil that is high in phosphorous and potassium. A fertilizer such as 8-24-24 used at the rate of 2 pounds per 100 square feet should be adequate as a pre-plant treatment. If your soil is tight it will probably be necessary to construct a raised bed for radishes, or at least work 2 to 4 inches of organic matter (pine bark, peat moss, compost, etc.) into the soil.

There are two types of radishes, differing in length of growing season. In the lower South radishes do best in the winter or when the temperatures are cool. Tough, pithy, hot radishes are produced during hot weather or when the radishes are slow to mature. Although not as successful in the summer, root crops, being intermediate in their light requirements, may be grown in partial shade in the summer with some success.

The small radish varieties should be spaced about an inch apart in the row with rows 14 to 24 inches apart. Large varieties, especially the oriental type, will need a spacing more like 4-6 inches in the row with rows 14 to 24 inches apart.

Recommended Varieties. The most popular radish types are the small round radishes, such as Cherry Bell and Early Scarlett Globe. There are also some rapid-maturing, relatively small, long-rooted types, such as White Icicle and Scarlett Icicle. The so-called winter varieties take much longer to mature and are usually best planted in the fall. Some of these attain extremely large size—one variety, called Sakurajima, reportedly grows to 50 pounds in the Orient. Nine to ten pound radishes are not unusual with this variety. What is unusual is that they are not hot and pithy, but are instead rather mild. They are good cooked with greens, hot peppers, bacon grease and a dash of vinegar. These radishes are also good stirred-fried in oriental dishes (this is called Daikon), or you can enjoy them raw. Other good winter varieties are Round Black Spanish, Long Black Spanish, Celestial and China Rose.

Harvesting. Radishes, because they develop partially out of the ground, are easy to know when to harvest. Just pull them when they appear the right size. If planted too thickly they can be thinned and the small radishes used in an immature stage. If allowed to get too large they soon become pithy.

Diseases. Diseases are no problem with radishes in southern home gardens.

Insects. Aphids can be a problem but are easily controlled. Flea beetles sometimes attack radishes, and there are root maggots which are bothersome and require both the application of a soil insecticide and crop rotation.

Spinach

History. Spinach probably originated in the Middle East and eventually spread from the Orient to Southern Europe and America. There are generally two types of spinach: the round-seeded varieties which are principally grown in the United States, and the prickly-seeded spinach with spiney seeds. The latter has more triangular leaves and is more spreading. It is still somewhat popular in the Orient.

Culture. Spinach is a long-day plant, meaning that it bolts to seed when the days lengthen in late spring and early summer. For this reason, spinach is best grown in the fall. Many varieties are slow to go to seed, but even these will not hold back for long in the spring. Plants should be thinned to stand 3 to 4 inches in the row with rows 14 to 24 inches apart.

Recommended Varieties: Long Standing Bloomsdale, Hybrid 7, Dixie Market, Virginia Savoy Hybrid, and Viroflay.

Harvesting. Spinach in the home garden should be harvested like other greens, by picking the outer leaves rather than harvesting the entire plant at one time.

Diseases. There are several diseases that bother spinach, in particular, downey mildew, various leaf-spotting fungal diseases, several viruses, and white rust. The use of resistant varieties, if available, is recommended for most of these diseases, with the exception of white rust, for which

fungicide applications are often helpful or absolutely necessary. Fungicide applications must begin when the first 3 to 4 leaves are about ¾ grown. Several subsequent applications will then be needed weekly. White rust appears as white, blister-like areas that initially form on the lower side of the leaf, eventually spreading to the upper side and often causing the leaves to appear yellow and chlorotic.

Insects. Spinach's major insect pest is the aphid. If populations of this insect build up in large numbers an insecticide may be necessary. High-pressure sprays of water may help to wash the insect pest loose.

Turnips

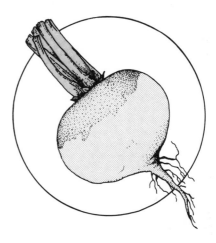

History. The turnip is reported to grow wild in northern Russia, but there is some speculation about its actual origin. It was brought to America in the early seventeenth century.

Culture. Turnips are typically thought of as root crops, but southerners often grow them as much for the tops or greens as for the root, and the two are often cooked together with the addition of other leafy vegetables. Turnips, as all root crops, need a loose soil, high in phosphorus and potassium but relatively low in nitrogen, unless production of tops is the main concern. Turnips should be spaced 2 to 3 inches apart in the row with rows 14 to 24 inches apart.

Recommended Varieties: for roots—Purple Top, White Globe, and the new quick-maturing white hybrid varieties like Tokyo Market Express; for greens—Seven Top and Shogoin.

Harvesting. Pick most turnip varieties when 2 to 3 inches in diameter. However, many of the new white oriental hybrids are best when only 1 to 1½ inches in diameter. Turnip greens should be picked while quite small (6 to 8 inches in length).

Diseases. Turnips are bothered by the same diseases that affect mustard—white rust, black rot,

bacterial leaf spot, and pollution damage (particularly sulfur dioxide).

Insects. Aphids, or plant lice, are turnips' primary insect pest. They are easily controlled with recommended insecticides. Root maggots may be more of a problem, but they can be controlled with soil applications of recommended insecticides. Flea beetles, which chew numerous small holes in the leaves, can also be damaging but are easily controlled.

Other cool season vegetables

• **Globe Artichokes** can be grown with some success in the lower South. Plant good strong divisions in the fall, in a rich organic soil much like you would use for asparagus. Red spiders and hot weather are the main limiting factors which may keep you from harvesting a few artichokes. Unfortunately even if you do harvest some they are three for a dollar in the supermarket anyway.

• **Cardoon,** a member of the thistle family, looks very much like the globe artichoke. Instead of being grown for the flower bud, however, this vegetable is grown for the leaf petioles, which are blanched (mounded with soil or wrapped with newspaper to exclude light) to make their flavor milder; they are bitter if this step is left out. The stalks are harvested, boiled, the tough outer skin is removed, and they are dipped in batter and fried. Plants do well in the lower South if planted in the fall.

• **Celery** is a major vegetable in some areas of the South, yet as a home garden vegetable it is lacking because it takes so long to mature (130 days). Seed should be started in August or September and transplanted to a rich prepared soil such as described for asparagus. Sidedressing each plant every 2 to 3 weeks with ammonium sulfate (21-0-0), one teaspoon per plant, may be necessary to ensure rapid growth. Even with this treatment, plants will be slow growing during cold cloudy days in the winter.

• **Chinese Cabbage** can mean different things to different people. It refers to two types of green vegetable. One is the heading type, the more compact, tightly wrapped Pe-Tsai cabbage rarely

grown by the home gardener; another heading type, the Chihli cabbage (Michihli var.), has more elongated heads less tightly wrapped. Though likely to go to seed if left too long when mature, these vegetables make an excellent addition to the southern home garden. The other leafy Oriental vegetable considered a member of the cabbage family is Pak-Choi, which looks like Swiss Chard. It is very easy to grow and delicious in stirred-fried dishes. The vast number of oriental green vegetables is impressive. Others worthy of trial are: Mizuna, Shirona and edible-leaved chrysanthemum.

• **Corn Salad** makes an interesting addition to the winter salad. Though considered a mild vegetable (and it is), it has an almost aromatic flavor. Grow like you would lettuce.

• **Cress.** There are several types of cress used as a substitute for watercress or for the pungency they add to salads. Particularly good is Garden Cress or Pepper Grass which is used in the sprout stage or while very young. It has a hot peppery flavor. Upland Cress is very similar to watercress but can be grown without running water. It requires a moist soil, however. Rocket is not a cress but it is used in much the same way, as an addition to salads. It grows very well in cool weather, bolting quickly to seed in the spring. Its flavor can best be described as a dirty sock dipped in hot horseradish mustard.

• **Salsify and Scorzonera** are root vegetables seldom grown in the home garden, and this neglect is probably justified. After the long thin roots are peeled, little is left to eat. Both need a rich, deep soil. Scorzonera has black-skinned roots and wider leaves than the Salsify or Oyster plant. The latter is supposed to resemble the taste of oysters.

● **Texsel** is a new leafy vegetable introduced by Texas A&M University. It is a member of the cabbage family, very prolific and easy to grow.

Asparagus, a perennial vegetable

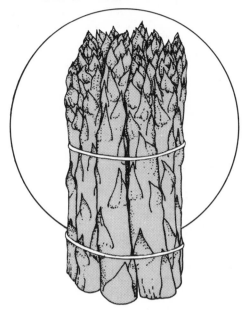

Yet asparagus can be grown well enough to justify its planting in many home gardens. It is a gourmet vegetable and one that is expensive to purchase at the store. It is a heavy feeder and needs a rich soil mixed with 2-4 inches of rotted mature. Apply fertilizer such as 12-12-12 several times a year, one application before growth starts in the spring and another as soon as harvesting is finished.

A Special Bed. Plant asparagus in raised beds if your soil is tight and rainfall is plentiful. Plants should be spaced 18 inches apart in the row, with rows 36 to 48 inches apart. Plant disease-resistant varieties such as Mary Washington.

When the stalks die in the fall they should be cut level with the ground, raked, and disposed of. Weeds are a problem in asparagus beds, and hand weeding the small bed is recommended. After harvesting, a mulch can effectively reduce weed problems.

History. Asparagus comes from Europe and Asia, where it has been grown for more than 2,000 years. The Greeks and Romans used asparagus not only as a food but for medicinal purposes also. This vegetable has been grown in the United States since the sixteenth century.

Culture. Asparagus is not well adapted to the lower South. It simply grows too much of the time, and as a result of the plant's brief-to-negligible dormancy here, it does not store much food. Thus, asparagus, particularly when grown in the lower South, does not produce the large, thick spears that it does in the North or in areas where an artificial dormancy can be induced by taking away irrigation water and subjecting the plants to a drought.

Harvesting. Asparagus should be allowed to grow for two seasons before you do any harvesting. The first year, harvest for 2 to 3 weeks, the second year 3 to 4 weeks, and in future years it should be possible to harvest for 6 to 8 weeks. Spears may either be cut 1 to 2 inches below the soil or snapped off.

Disease. The major disease problem is a rust. Planting resistant varieties is the main control.

Insects. Asparagus beetles may sometimes damage plantings. Recommended insecticides can be used to control this pest as well as cutworms, snails, and slugs.

Swiss chard, a year-round vegetable

History. Swiss Chard is a variety of beet that does not form a root. Beets are probably natives of Europe. Their appearance in America was first documented in 1806.

Culture. Swiss Chard is one of our few truly year-round vegetables. It tolerates all but the coldest, dry wind in winter and does well in summer heat, too. Swiss Chard is one of the few vegetables that demands a neutral or slightly alkaline soil, so liming may be necessary. It also responds to the addition of a generous quantity of organic matter, especially something like rotted manure. Like all leafy vegetables, it has a fairly high demand for nitrogen and appreciates several sidedressings with a nitrogen fertilizer during the growing season. Plants should be spaced 6 inches apart in the row, with rows 18 to 30 inches apart.

Recommended Varieties: There are few varieties of Swiss Chard to select from. The most readily available are Lucullus and Burgundy. The latter is a red-veined variety. A less well-known variety that makes luxuriant growth is called French Swiss Chard.

Harvesting. Swiss Chard should be harvested by cutting or breaking off the outer leaves when they are approximately 12 to 18 inches tall. If this is done regularly, plants can be harvested over a long period of time. Leaves that get too large and develop tough petioles should be used for the leafy portion only.

Diseases and Insects. Disease problems are minor and no spraying should be necessary. Insects, especially caterpillars, sometimes chew a few holes in the leaves, but this usually is not worth treating for. If cabbage loopers (little green inch worms) become a nuisance one of the new biological sprays containing a bacterium that sickens and eventually kills the caterpillar can be used safely in the home garden. Since these materials are sensitive to ultraviolet light, it is best to spray in the evening or in the early morning.

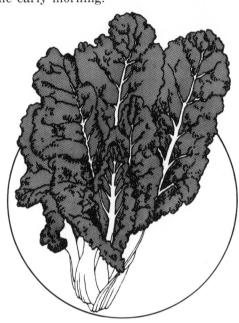

Warm Season Vegetables

Beans

History. Snapbeans are native to South America and were cultivated by the American Indians before they were generally grown in Europe.

Culture. By far, the most popular bean for Southern home gardens is the bush snapbean. It is very productive, tasty, and nutritious. While pole snapbeans do well in the spring garden, the bush snapbean thrives in both the spring and fall garden.

Bush snapbeans are best planted every two weeks to mature before or after midsummer temperatures get too hot. Expect July and August to be months of little production for beans. The first fall frost also halts production, but the excellent quality beans produced during cool weather prior to the frost are worth the disappointment.

Beans, being legumes, produce much of the nitrogen they need from the air with the help of *Rhizobium* bacteria. Small home garden packets of *Rhizobium* innoculant are available from seed companies, and use of this material is recommended. The bacteria form nodules on the roots, and through a biochemical process, convert gaseous nitrogen into a form they can use. Ultimately, they release this nitrogen to the plants. Applying 1 to 2 pounds of 6-24-24 or a similar analysis fertilizer per 100 sqaure feet should be adequate for most soils.

Bean sprouts lift much of the bulk of the seed out of the soil during germination, so the seed is especially sensitive to being planted too deep. In tight soils plant the seed no deeper than 1 inch and no deeper than 1½ inches in sandy soils; if planted deeper the plants will be stunted if they come up at all. When planting in tight soils, cover the seed with a half-and-half mixture of compost and sand or just sand.

Recommended Varieties: Bush snapbean varieties for the South include: Contender, Provider, Spartan Arrow, Topcrop and Astro.

Harvesting. Snap Beans should be harvested before the seed begins to swell noticeably in the pod. At this stage the beans will snap readily.

Diseases. Although several diseases attack beans, many of the new varieties are resistant to them. Leaf-spotting diseases, caused by fungi and bacteria, can usually be avoided by planting disease-free seed. Most good bean seed is grown in the West, where these diseases don't occur. A rust disease, which looks like you might expect—small reddish-brown pustules on the underside of the leaves is sometimes a problem. This disease overwinters on old crop residue and can best be controlled by rotation, although regular dusting with sulfur is also effective.

Powdery mildew is sometimes a problem. Dusting with sulfur will help control this disease.

Damping-off can be a problem with germinating seedlings, especially in the spring when soils are cool. Planting treated seed and waiting until the soil warms up lessens the severity of this disease.

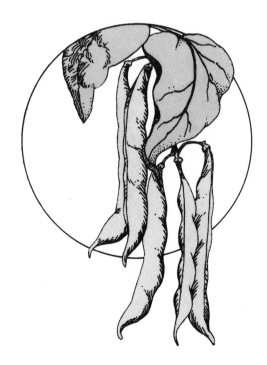

Insects. Beans' major pest is really not an insect, it is an arachnid—the red spider mite. The symptom is yellow stippled areas on the leaves, which eventually drop. Control with an insecticide requires at least three sprays three days apart (see page 48). Sulfur also provides some control.

Chewing insects, such as the Mexican Bean Beetle, can also do great damage, but these pests are relatively easy to control.

Pole Snapbeans

Pole beans originated in the same part of Southern or Central America as the bush bean. They require essentially the same cultivation as bush beans except that, obviously, they need some type of trellis such as a chain link fence. Plants should be thinned to stand 4 to 6 inches apart in the row, with rows 36 to 48 inches apart. The best overall variety is Kentucky Wonder. There is also a Kentucky Wonder wax bean, and there are several other green varieties worth trying, including Dade, McCaslan, and Blue Lake. Pole beans can be very productive in a relatively small space. They are restricted to the spring garden in most areas of the South because they require a relatively long growing season. Disease and insect pests are the same as for bush bean varieties.

Bush Lima Beans

History. It was once thought that lima beans originated in Africa, but they are now believed to be of tropical American origin. They were probably indigenous to Guatemala, from whence they were widely distributed until pre-Columbian times. There are two basic categories of lima beans—the large-seeded and the small-seeded, both of which belong to a single species.

Culture. Limas are a little more difficult to grow than snapbeans. They will not germinate in as cool a soil, nor will they set fruit when temperatures approach 90°. For these reasons, and because they must be shelled and produce less edible food for the amount of area involved, they are less popular than snapbeans. Bush limas should be spaced 3 to 4 inches in the row, with rows 30 to 36 inches apart.

Recommended Varieties: Henderson's Bush and Jackson Wonder.

Harvesting. Lima Beans, peas, and other green-shelled beans are best picked when plump but still bright green.

Diseases and Insects: These pests are similar to those that attack green beans.

Pole Lima Beans

Pole beans require the same general care that bush limas do. Plants should be spaced 12 to 18 inches in the row, with rows 36-48 inches apart. Recommended varieties include Carolina Sieva and Florida Butter.

Sweet corn

History. Corn was a leading crop among Indians in America about the time this continent was discovered. Its exact place of origin in the Americas is unknown, and it was a good number of years before Sweet Corn (as opposed to Field Corn) was mentioned in American literature. By the middle of the nineteenth century it had been frequently mentioned, however. The so-called Indian, or Ornamental, Corn varieties are undoubtedly similar to ancient corn types grown by the Indians. These cannot compare in flavor to new hybrid Sweet Corn varieties.

Culture. Sweet Corn is not well-adapted to the small garden because several rows must be planted to insure good pollination. When only one row is planted the result is likely to be magnificent cobs but little corn. Corn requires a considerable amount of fertilizer. At planting time, work 2 to 3 pounds of 12-24-12 or a similar analysis fertilizer into 100 square feet of garden area. When the corn is 6 to 8 inches high begin sidedressing with 1 to 1½ pounds of ammonium sulfate (21-0-0) per 100 feet of row and throw 6 to 8 inches of soil up to the base of the plants. Support roots will grow into this soil. Two to three sidedressings of fertilizer should be adequate. Plants should be spaced 12 to 18 inches apart in the row, with rows 24 to 36 inches apart.

Recommended Varieties: Valley Market, Merit, Golden Security, Seneca Chief, Aristogold Hybrid, Bonanza, and Buttersweet. Silver Queen is an excellent white corn variety. Many southerners like a large-eared variety for roasting. Hybrid Trucker's Favorite is one of the better varieties of this type of corn.

Harvesting. If you are to get the greatest benefit from growing your own corn it is important to harvest it properly and prepare it immediately (within a couple of hours). The highest quality sweet corn is harvested in the milk stage. At this point the kernels, when punctured with a thumbnail, have a milky exudate. If a doughy material comes out the corn is too ripe. Harvested sweet corn should be brought in immediately and soaked in ice water until cooked and served.

Diseases. A number of diseases attack corn, including seedling blights (damping-off), smut, mildew, leaf blights, viruses, etc. Few of these diseases require control in the home garden except for damping-off, which the use of fungicide-treated seed will help to eliminate.

Insects. The corn earworm is Sweet Corn's most serious pest in the South. It is almost impossible to harvest complete ears of corn unless insecticide is applied regularly during the period of silk formation. The southern corn rootworm can also be damaging, especially to young plants. This pest is the larva of the 12-spotted cucumber beetle. The larve damage the plants by feeding on the roots, eventually boring through the crown to reach the bud. You may need to apply soil insecticides if this pest has been a problem in the past.

Cucumber

History. The cucumber has been cultivated for thousands of years. It is probably a native of Asia or Africa and may date back at least 3,000 years.

Culture. Cucumbers need to be grown in a loose, fertile soil that has warmed up thoroughly. Most varieties do very well in the home garden when grown on a fence. Plants should be spaced 24 to 48 inches in the row, with rows 48 to 72 inches apart.

Recommended Varieties: There are many cucumber varieties adapted to the South, including new hybrids that come out every year. Varieties recommended by your State Agricultural Extension Service should constitute the bulk of your planting, but by all means try some of the new hybrids and some of the more unusual types. Standard varieties include: Pickling types—Pioneer, Salty, Ohio MR 17, Chipper, SMR 58 and Piccadilly; Slicing types—Poinsett, Cherokee 7, Ashley, Tex-Long, and Polaris. Some unusual varieties worth trying include: Burpless Hybrid, Yamato, Yard-Long, Kaga, and several other long cucumbers which need to be grown on a fence. There's a lemon cucumber which is delicious, though it doesn't taste much like a lemon. It is also burpless. There is also a white cucumber, White Wonder, and a small cucumber from the West Indies, called a gerkin, that makes delicious pickles. Although varieties are usually recommended for slicing or pickling, their uses overlap quite a bit. For instance, the long Japanese or Burpless cucumbers make excellent chip pickles. They can also be used to make dill pickles, but an 18-inch dill pickle, in addition to being cumbersome at the table, is rather difficult to squeeze into a quart jar.

Harvesting. Cucumbers for sweet pickles should be picked when 2 to 3 inches long; for dill pickles, pick when 4 to 6 inches long. Slicing varieties are usually allowed to reach 6 to 8 inches in length, though the burpless hybrid types may easily be a foot long at the best stage for harvesting. Frequent picking is necessary to prevent cucumbers from going to seed, which reduces the productivity of the vines.

Diseases. Cucumbers, cantaloupes, squash, and pumpkins suffer most of the same diseases. Downey mildew is common and appears as yellow spots on the upper surface of the leaf, while the underside of the leaf opposite the yellow spots becomes covered with a grayish growth. Powdery mildew appears as a white powder and is found on the upper surface of the leaf. Anthracnose disease causes yellowish spots that eventually enlarge and rot out, giving the leaf a shot-hole appearance. Gummy-stem blight affects the leaves and stems, usually at the crown of the plant.

Virus diseases cause mottling and distortion, along with discoloration of the fruit. Fruit rot is one of the most serious diseases. Many new varieties are resistant to one or several of these diseases, and seed catalog descriptions usually indicate this. Chemical fungicides can also be used, but be sure to note and observe the harvest interval (time between spray application and harvesting). Spacing the plants adequately improves air considerably. The severity of this disease can also be reduced by removing diseased fruit as soon as it is noticed and by using a mulch.

Insects. Several insect pests attack squash, including the spotted or striped cucumber beetles that eat holes in the leaves of young plants. These pests also attack a wide variety of other plants, and they sometimes feed on the flowers. They are difficult to control because they are rather mobile, and regular applications of an insecticide will be required. The squash vine borer is a common pest. Its larvae tunnel into the stems of plants, eventually causing them to wilt. In the early stages a razor blade can sometimes be used to puncture the insect, after which soil is mounded over the damaged stem, allowing it to form new roots. Regular insecticide applications can prevent this pest from getting into the plants in the first place. Pre-planting soil applications of an insecticide are not effective in preventing attack. The adult is an orange moth that lays eggs on the stem; thus, little actual contact with the soil is made. Spider mites may also give you some trouble.

Eggplant

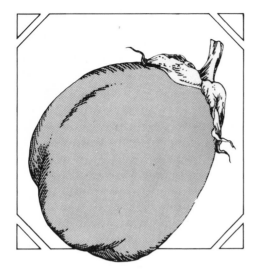

History. The eggplant is a native of tropical India. There are three general types of eggplant: the large-fruited type, which is by far the most popular in the United States; the long, thin eggplants commonly called Oriental or Italian types; and small-fruited eggplants often used for pickling.

Culture. The eggplant is ideally suited to the South because it requires a long, warm growing season. If planted too early in the spring, when the soil and night temperatures are cool, eggplant may be stunted and refuse to grow, even after the soil warms up. Like the tomato and pepper, eggplant produces a large plant and little fruit if fertilized with too much nitrogen. Therefore, a 6-24-24 or similar analysis fertilizer is best to use prior to planting, adding supplemental nitrogen (1 tablespoon per 2-foot of row) once fruit set has begun. Plants should be spaced 18 to 24 inches in the row, with rows 24 to 36 inches apart.

Recommended Varieties: large-fruited types—Black Beauty Hybrid and Florida Market. (Cooks Strain); Oriental or long-fruited types—Chinese Long and Long Tom; small-fruited types—Short Tom. A number of other varieties are available, including green, white (White Beauty), and golden eggplants.

Harvesting. Eggplant should be harvested anytime between half maturity and the point where it begins to loose its gloss. Overly mature fruits are usually bitter and seedy.

Diseases. Fruit rot is one of the main home garden disease problems with eggplants. It is best prevented by planting resistant varieties such as Florida Market.

Insects. Many of the same insects that attack tomatoes and peppers also attack eggplants. Perhaps the most serious pest, though not an insect, is the red spider mite. Spraying a miticide at three-day intervals will be necessary to control this pest. Flea beetles, aphids, and a lace bug may also attack eggplants.

Cantaloupe (Muskmelon)

History. Cantaloupes have never been found growing wild, but they probably originated in Asia. In the United States cantaloupes were recorded in 1609 in Virginia. What is commonly grown is actually not a cantaloupe, it is a muskmelon. A true cantaloupe produces warty, rough, hard-rinded fruit, and it is practically unknown in the United States.

Culture. Cantaloupes (muskmelons) require too much space for most home gardens, but they can be grown easily on a fence. Plants should be spaced 24 to 36 inches in the row, with rows 60 to 96 inches apart.

Recommended Varieties: Perlita, Smith's Perfect, Israeli (Oghen Melon), Casaba, and Crenshaw.

Harvesting. The stem of the muskmelon should slip or break easily from the fruit for maximum quality in the home garden. In addition, the opposite end of the fruit should have begun to soften, and some melons, especially the Crenshaw and Persian varieties, develop a strong, fruity aroma at the blossom end.

Diseases and Insects: Pests of the muskmelon are similar to those of the cucumber, squash, and pumpkin.

Okra

History. Okra is related to cotton and is thought to be of African or Asiatic origin. It is primarily a southern vegetable and its culture and uses are only casually mentioned in most garden books written for the North. Okra has been mentioned as growing in the United States as early as 1748.

Okra is used in soups known as gumbos, and it is especially delicious as a fried vegetable coated with a cornmeal batter and mixed with tomatoes.

Culture. Okra is very sensitive to cold, especially cold soils. Don't be in a hurry to plant okra. The seed is relatively hard so soak it overnight to hasten germination. Okra plants should be thinned to stand 24 inches apart in the row, with rows 36 to 42 inches apart. Okra is one of the few vegetables that seems to grow better in a tight soil.

Recommended Varieties: Emerald, Louisiana Green Velvet, Clemson Spineless, White Velvet, and a dwarf variety, Gold Coast. An edible ornamental type called Red River has bright red pods, leaf veins, petioles, and stems.

Harvesting. Okra needs to be harvested regularly, at least every 2 to 3 days. Although some varieties get much larger before they become woody, it is best to pick okra while small. If pods are allowed to mature seed, production will be severely reduced.

Diseases. Few diseases trouble okra. Fusariam Wilt sometimes causes damage, and the only control is to rotate crops. Root knot nematodes are also a problem, and they are probably best controlled with nematacide used prior to planting. Nematodes seem to be worse in sandy soils than they are in clay soils. Fruit rot may also be a minor problem.

Insects. Okra's main pests are sucking insects of the true bug family, including the stinkbug and the leaf-footed bug. This latter insect has a leaf-like appendage on its hind legs. Because okra is a minor crop (except in the South) few pesticides have been thoroughly tested and recommended for use on it. Hand picking these insect pests will probably be necessary in the home garden. Pods that have been attacked by either of these two pests appear curled, distorted, or may have bumpy or pimpled areas.

Southern peas

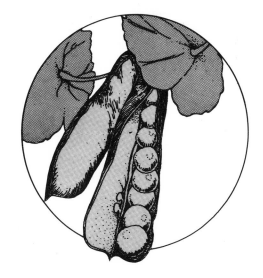

History. Southern peas originated in Africa and grow wild there still. As the name suggests, this vegetable is grown primarily in the South. Southern peas may be used as a shelled bean (green or dry), and some types are used as snapbeans while young and tender. A climbing variety, the Yardlong Bean, is very popular with Orientals. As with other legumes, southern peas contain plenty of protein, and so, are very nutritious.

Culture. Southern peas require warm soil. Plants should be spaced 4 to 6 inches apart in the row, with rows 24 to 36 inches apart.

Recommended Varieties: One of the most promising varieties is Mississippi Silver. This variety is resistant to Fusariam Wilt and nematodes. Other good varieties are Blackeye No. 5, Purple Hull, Queen Ann, Brown Sugar Crowder, Cream 40, and Champion.

Harvesting. Southern Peas should be harvested before the pods begin to turn yellow and while the seed is still tender and juicy. Peas may also be allowed to mature to be used as dry shelled beans.

Diseases. There are a number of diseases that attack southern peas, including: Powdery Mildew, Fusariam Wilt, Rust, Leaf Spot, Southern Blight, Ashy Stem Blight, Damping-off, Bacterial Blight, Mosaic Virus, Cotton Root Rot, and Nematodes. These diseases usually are not much of a problem in the home garden, except where peas have been grown continuously for some time.

Insects. A number of chewing insects attack southern peas. Most of these are easily controlled. One of the most difficult pests is the green stinkbug (the leaf-footed bug). This pest sucks the juices out of the peas and may inhibit their development. Green stinkbugs are difficult to control because relatively few pesticides are cleared for use on southern peas. Bean weevils may also cause damage.

Peppers

History. Peppers (not including black pepper, which is the seed of the tropical vine, *Piper nigrum*) are new world vegetables. Once discovered by Columbus, the pepper became widely popular in Europe via Spain. It became so common in India that for awhile some botanists thought it to be native to that region. The first peppers grown in the United States probably came from Europe rather than from their place of origin in Central or South America.

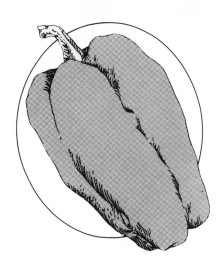

Culture. Peppers are more demanding in their cultural needs than tomatoes. They require a very moderate temperature, and won't grow when temperatures get too cool (below 60°) or too warm (90°F or above). Initially, they may need more nitrogen than tomatoes—if a pepper plant begins setting peppers when it is less than a foot tall, the small peppers should be removed and the plant sidedressed with about 1 tablespoon of ammonium sulfate to encourage more foliage production and, thus, larger peppers. This extra fertilizer is usually necessary with the bell pepper varieties. Plants should be spaced 18 to 24 inches apart in the row, with rows 24 to 36 inches apart.

Recommended Varieties: Bell types—Yolo Wonder, Canape, Keystone Resistant Giant; other sweet pepper types—Yellow Banana; mildly pungent varieties—College 64L, Anaheim Chile; hot pepper varieties—Cayenne, Tabasco, Fresno Chile, Serrano Chile, Hungarian Wax, and Jalapeno.

Harvesting. Peppers should be harvested whenever they are long enough to use. It is important to avoid leaving peppers on the plant too long after maturing, as this may reduce yields considerably.

Diseases. A number of leaf-spotting and fruit-rotting organisms can damage peppers. Most will be of minor concern in the home garden if you follow a weekly pesticide program. One disease, Southern Blight, is particularly troublesome and attacks the stem of the plant near the soil line, causing the plant to wilt and die. Southern Blight infection is evidenced by white cotton-like growth near the surface of the stem. It is difficult to control chemically, but deep plowing or otherwise turning the disease organism deep into the soil will help.

There are a number of mosaic virus diseases that attack members of the tomato, pepper, and eggplant family. There are no chemical controls for these diseases, but resistant varieties are being developed. One virus-resistant variety is Canape.

Insects. Flea beetles and leaf miners can cause considerable damage to young pepper plants. Leaf miners, the larvae of small gnat-sized flies, tunnel between the cell layers of leaves. Good control of these pests requires weekly spray applications.

Sweet potatoes

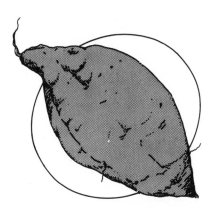

History. Sweet potatoes originated in South America. They are often mistakenly called yams, but the two plants are not closely related. The sweet potato was introduced into a number of Pacific Islands and New Zealand, as well as some of the Polynesian Islands. Columbus found sweet potato being used as food in Cuba, and they were grown in the United States in Virginia as early as 1648. The sweet potato is closely related to the Morning Glory, though it rarely blooms unless grown for long periods with low fertility.

Culture. Sweet potatoes do best in a sandy soil. Good drainage is necessary, and heavy clay soils cause roots to be rough and irregular. Sweet potatoes require a large garden. They are propagated by bedding healthy, disease-free roots in a hotbed or coldframe and covering these with sand. As the potatoes sprout, pull off and plant the so-called slips. Plants should be set 12 to 16 inches apart in the row, with rows 36 to 48 inches apart.

A low-nitrogen fertilizer such as 5-10-10 or 6-24-24 should be used to deter rank top growth which means few potatoes. This fertilizer is best applied two weeks prior to setting the slips. The slips should be set on high, ridge-style beds. Potatoes should be dug in the fall when they have reached the desired size.

Recommended Varieties: Centennial, Gold Rush, Puerta Rico, Rose Centennial, Julian, All Gold, Red Gold, and many others.

Harvesting. The best way to tell if sweet potatoes are ready is to do a little digging and look for mature roots. This will occur in summer or early fall prior to the first frost. If you leave potatoes in the ground during a hard freeze, dig them up as soon as possible afterwards. Avoid damaging roots when digging, and place them in baskets or boxes without cleaning or washing them.

Diseases. A number of diseases attack sweet potatoes, and most are associated with the soil. These include: Black Rot, Stem Rot, Scurf, Pox, Root Rot, Southern Blight (see peppers), and nematodes.

Insects. Sweet potatoes' most serious insect pest is the sweet potato weevil. The sweet potato weevil is spread by importation or planting of infested tubers for slip production. Chemical controls are used, but the use of long lasting chlorinated hydrocarbons may be prohibited in the future.

Pumpkin and Squash

History. Pumpkins were grown by early Indian tribes, probably having been brought as far north as New England from Central and South America. Many of the squash will cross with the pumpkin, and thus they probably originated from the same area.

Culture. Pumpkins need to be spaced 36 to 48 inches apart in the row, with rows 60 to 96 inches apart. They appreciate a slight amount of shade, and for this reason they are often grown together with corn or pole beans.

Don't be disappointed if the pumpkin you planted for a Halloween Jack-O-Lantern matures for the Fourth of July. They do best if planted in March, and when planted at that time they are ready in June or July. Try having turkey and dressing with pumpkin pie for your Fourth of July picnic. After all, 200 years is alot to be thankful for!

Recommended Varieties: New England Sugar, Jackpot, Funny Face. There are also large, relatively inedible varieties grown for show, such as Big Max. Squash varieties include the summer bush types, which need to be thinned to 18 to 36 inches apart in the row, with rows 36 to 60 inches apart. The winter squash varieties, which are generally vining types best adapted to a chain link fence in the small garden, need to be planted 24 to 48 inches apart in the row, with rows 60 to 96 inches apart. Summer squash varieties include: Gold Neck Hybrid, Dixie Hybrid, White Scallop, Zucco Zuchinni. Winter squash varieties: Acorn, Table Queen, or a bush variety, Table King, Butternut (var. Waltham). A low-nitrogen fertilizer such as 8-24-24 is good for pre-plant treatment to avoid excessive vegetation. Two pounds per 100 sq ft. is sufficient.

Harvesting. Pumpkins should be harvested when the skin is tough and has a deep, rich color. Summer squash varieties should be picked as follows: Yellow varieties, while still a light yellow in color; Scallop varieties, while they still have a greenish tint; Zuchinni, while small and tender (6 to 8 inches long). If Zuchinni is allowed to get large it can be cut open and the seeds removed for baking much like you would do with winter squash varieties. Winter varieties such as Acorn and Butternut should be left on the vine until the skin is tough and resistant to scratching with a thumb nail.

Diseases. The same leaf-spotting organisms that attack cucumbers will attack squash. One of the worst diseases is fruit rot. Soon after pollination, small fruit develop a black, whiskery growth. Chemical sprays give some control, but cultural methods are also important. A mulch over the soil area will help prevent transmission of the disease innoculum and keep the fruit off of the soil. Be sure to space the plants adequately for air circulation. As soon as fruit rot is noticed remove and destroy the infected fruit. Some gardeners cut out two or three of the older large leaves in the center of the plant to allow better air circulation and light penetration.

Insects. The same pests that attack cucumbers are a problem with squash. Mainly, the vine borer (this is especially a problem with squash and pumpkin), Squash bugs, leaf miners, and spotted or striped cucumber beetles. Regular spraying will be necessary to control these pests.

Watermelon

History. The watermelon originated in Africa and was introduced into the United States as early as 1629.

Culture. Watermelons require a great deal of space. Except for some of the small-fruited, more compact vines, they are not adapted to most home gardens. When planted in the home garden they should be spaced 36 to 72 inches apart in the row, with rows 72 to 96 inches apart. Recommended Varieties: Charleston Gray, Sugar Baby, Klondike, Seedless Tri-X 313, Crimson Sweet, Sweet Princess, and Yellow Baby. A number of new hybrid home garden varieties are worth a try.

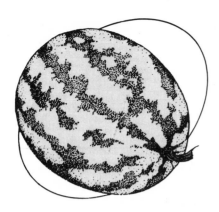

Harvesting. Determining when watermelons are ready to pick is quite an art. If it makes a thump when tapped with knuckles it is probably ready. If you get a higher pitched response it is probably not ready. The sure sign of ripeness for most varieties is the color of the underside of melon, where it has been lying on the ground. The melon is probably ripe after turning from a light to a deep yellow or gold.

Diseases. Several leaf-spotting diseases can damage watermelons, but one of the most serious diseases in the South is Fusarium Wilt, a soil-born disease. The only control is to plant resistant varieties such as Charleston Gray 133, and Smokylee.

Insects. Watermelon is troubled by the same insect pests that attack cucumbers, squash, etc. Aphids, too, may be particularly troublesome.

Tomatoes

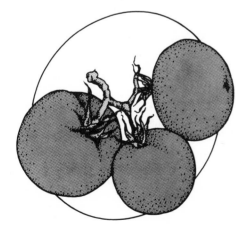

History. Without doubt, the tomato is the most popular home garden vegetable. The tomato, like the pepper and the potato, is strictly an American continent vegetable, having originated in Central and South America but introduced into the United States via Europe.

The tomato was first mentioned in Italy in the mid 16th century, and in the United States Thomas Jefferson suggested its use as a food in 1781. Until 1835 the tomato was grown more for ornament than food. The scientific name suggests less than a delicious vegetable—*Lycopersicon* means wolf peach and probably refers to the supposed poisonous qualities of this vegetable. As late as January 9, 1897, learned men of the day cautioned against eating tomatoes, as the following quote from the British publication, *The Gardener's Magazine*, attests:

> "The Tomato is once again being brought before the public as food to be avoided. Not long since we were assured that tomatoes produced cancer in those who ate them, but this slander proved to be unfounded. Now, according to Dr. W.T. English, of the Pennsylvania University, tomato eaters will be subject to a kind of heart disease. A steady use of the fruit is likely to produce organic and functional trouble; the sufferer gasps for breath, and has palpitations. We are glad the learned doctor thinks such poisoning will not kill save in rare cases."

The tomato is, of course, now known to be a very nutritious vegetable that causes *no ill effects* when eaten.

Culture. In the South tomatoes are rarely grown without some type of support. They may be staked, caged, or planted around rings of compost (Japanese Tomato Ring), but they are rarely left to lay on the ground because this exposes them to disease in the South. Plants grown without support should be mulched to minimize ground contact. Plants should be spaced 18-36 inches apart in the row, with rows 24-48 inches apart.

One common error is to use a fertilizer with too much nitrogen early in the growing stage. You end up with an 8-foot tomato bush and no tomatoes. Use only superphosphate (0-20-0 or 0-46-0), 2-5 pounds per 100 square feet, as a pre-plant incorporation in the soil. (To start, 8-24-24 can also be used.) Once the plants have set tomatoes the size of a dime, begin sidedressing with 1 tablespoon of ammonium sulfate (21-0-0) per 2 feet of row. Apply the fertilizer 8-12 inches to the side of the plant, and water it in. Continue every two to three weeks.

Recommended Varieties. Tomatoes are available in a great many forms, colors, and sizes. There are red, orange, pink, yellow, striped, and white tomatoes. Some are round, others are pear-shaped. There are acid tomatoes, bland tomatoes, juicy ones, and some that are downright mealy. In short, there is an extensive number of varieties available, both standard and hybrid types. Even if you choose the varieties recommended by your State Agricultural Extension Service, and often these aren't available unless you grow your own from seed, the results will vary from year to year. Chances are you'll always be testing new tomato varieties. Some good varieties for the South include: Canning tomatoes—Chico III and Roma; standard varieties (these can also be canned)—Homestead 24, Early Giant Hybrid, Floradel, Traveler, and Spring Giant, Terrific, Walter, Better Boy, and Early Girl.

Harvesting. For maximum flavor, home garden tomatoes should be allowed to mature to red ripeness on the vine. They may be picked with some green still evident and ripened indoors, but they won't have the outstanding flavor of fully vine-ripened tomatoes. Allowing fruits to ripen completely (even a little overripe) is very important if you plan to can tomatoes.

Diseases. Tomatoes are plagued by several leaf-spotting diseases that can be prevented with a general purpose garden fungicide. Once the leaves are visibly spotted, however, it's too late. The threat from pests such as Fusarium wilt and nem-todes can be offset by selecting resistant varieties. The letters VFN following the name of a variety denote resistance to Verticillium Wilt, Fusarium Wilt, and nematodes.

Insects. Insect pests are numerous. One of the most devastating is the tomato hornworm. It can almost eat a plant overnight. If you inspect your plants carefully you'll probably be able to pick them off and destroy them while they're young. Try spraying with the new bacterial spray *(Bacillus thuringiensis)* that sickens and eventually kills the caterpillar.

Other pests aren't disposed of so easily. Leaf miners leave wiggly tracks all through the leaves, eventually damaging them severely. The leaf miner, the larvae of a small fly, tunnels between the cell layers. The adult flies must be killed; it's difficult to kill the larvae because they are well protected between the plant cells. Regular spraying is necessary to stave off these fellows.

Cutworms are easy to thwart by placing a barrier between the worm and the stem. This might be a cardboard collar, waxpaper collar, an old milk carton with the bottom cut out, or a styrofoam "hot cup" torn open at the bottom to allow the plant to grow through.

Stinkbugs suck juices out of the developing fruit, killing some of the cells and resulting in a yellowed area on the shoulder of the fruit. The fruit underneath this area is pithy and white. Stinkbugs are difficult to control; if chemical sprays fail, hand picking may be necessary.

Japanese tomato ring

One hundred pounds of tomatoes from a circular area 7 feet in diameter. You can do it, with a Japanese Tomato Ring. First, find a 7-foot spot in the sun. Then scrape off the existing groundcover and dig 2-4 inches of organic matter (peat moss, pine bark, etc.) plus 5 pounds of superphosphate (0-20-0) per 100 square feet into the top 6 inches of soil over the entire circular area. Use 5-20-20, or similar analysis fertilizer, if you can't find superphosphate.

You'll also need:

15 feet of wire fence (it needs to be sturdier than chicken wire, with small openings), use less for a smaller ring and fewer tomato plants.

4 sturdy, rot-resistant stakes 6-7 feet long
4 bales of hay (check with local farmers, they may have some that has been rained on or otherwise spoiled) or use other coarse organic refuse like corn stalks.
10 pints (lbs) of 12-24-12 or similar analysis fertilizer (1 pint = approximately 1 pound)
2 cubic yards of top soil
2 cubic yards of pine bark, rice hulls, well-rotted manure or compost (4 cubic yards of compost can be substituted for the combination of soil and organic matter)
plastic tape or soft cloth for ties
4 tomato plants (Early Girl, Better Boy, Homestead 24 or Early Giant Hybrid) *(Continued)*

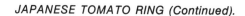

JAPANESE TOMATO RING (Continued).

Form the wire into a cylinder about 5 feet in diameter and anchor it to the ground with the stakes. Use the hay to line the inside of the ring—this will prevent the finer materials from sifting out of the wire. At the bottom of the cylinder put a 6-inch layer of organic matter followed by a 6-inch layer of soil etc, until you reach the top of the ring. As you work your way up don't forget to line the cylinder with hay.

Finish the ring with a layer of soil, dish-shaped to hold water, and 2 pounds of fertilizer. If you really want to do it right, mix the fertilizer uniformly with the soil and organic matter as you construct the ring.

Plant your tomato plants around the outside of the ring and water them in. As the plants get larger, concentrate the water in the top of the ring. This will wash valuable minerals and nutrients into the tomato plants' root zone.

As the plants grow tie them to the outside of the ring. They will completely cover the cylinder before you know it. Once the plants are set out, spray weekly with a combination vegetable garden insecticide/fungicide. Be sure to observe label recommendations and harvest intervals between spraying and picking. Apply another 2 pounds of fertilizer about every 3 weeks. The tomato ring can be saved and used over and over again.

There are several possible reasons for the phenomenal growth and production this ring promotes. It may be because the organic leachates filter down into the root zone, perhaps encouraging beneficial microorganisms; or it may be that a higher concentration of CO_2 accumulates around the leaves because of the decomposing organic matter, and this vital raw material of photosynthesis encourages better growth. Whatever the reason, you'll be amazed and delighted. If you don't think you can eat 100 pounds of tomatoes, cut the size and recommended materials in half.

Early in the year (February) use the top part of the ring and the area between the tomato plants to grow onions, potatoes, or long Oriental radishes (daikon) like White Celestial. Plant snow peas (edible podded peas) between the tomatoes at the base of the ring, and plan to plant these all around the ring again in the fall. Sweet peas are another possibility. By the time the tomatoes cover the ring these crops will be finished.

Caged Tomatoes

The days of staked tomatoes are rapidly fading. One of the best ways to keep tomatoes up off the ground, clean and free of diseases, is with a wire cage. The wire for this cage (cylinder) should be fairly sturdy. Six-inch mesh reinforcing wire is ideal, but "hog wire" can be used if it is supported with several stakes. A 5-foot section about 5 feet long can be bent into a 19-inch diameter cylinder.

By snipping off the bottom rung you create wire spikes that help to hold the cage in place over the plant. In addition, use some type of peg to further secure the ring.

From here the plant just grows up through the ring. Don't worry about tying or pruning it, just let it grow. The fruit will be shaded so there's less chance of sunscald, the plant is easy to spray and the fruit is easy to pick. After the soil has warmed up in the spring use an organic mulch such as spoiled hay to conserve moisture and stifle weeds.

Fertilizer Cans

Another technique that works well with tomatoes, caged or otherwise, is to place gallon cans in the ground for fertilizer and water resevoirs. Sink the cans in the soil, allowing 1 inch to stick up above the surface of the soil. Before putting the cans in, punch 6 or 7 holes in the side at the bottom with a can opener. Use two cans per plant with one can at each end of the row.

When tomatoes in the first cluster of fruit are the size of a dime begin adding 1 to 2 tablespoons of a complete fertilizer to each can each week. Of course, water the plants by filling the cans as needed (usually 2-3 times per week when they are bearing).

Other warm season vegetables

Variety is the spice of life, and vegetable gardens. Everyone has a special variety or different kind of vegetable that they like to pass around to fellow gardeners. In the South we are blessed with a mild climate that allows us to grow a wide variety of exotic vegetables. Our northern neighbors may have rhubarb, but we have yard-long beans, climbing okra, climbing spinach, edible soybeans chayote, and many others. Here are some unusual warm season vegetables that you may want to try in your garden.

● **Yard-long beans (Asparagus beans).** There are at least three varieties of this relative of the black-eyed pea. It is used more often as a snapbean than as a shell bean, and it is especially good in oriental dishes. Pick beans when 12 inches long or less or they may be tough. Since it requires a long growing season, it is particularly adapted to the South, and because of its vigorous growth it should be grown on a trellis or fence. The varieties are: Extra Long Red Seeded, the most common type; Extra Long Black-Seeded, longer, more tender and deeper green than the red-seeded; and Chinese Yard-Long, similar to the red-seeded variety, but the seed is tipped with white and the pod, though shorter, is often set in pairs.

● **Climbing Okra.** This vegetable may be one of several gourds, either a Luffa or a Lagenaria. The former, the so-called vegetable sponge, is available in a smooth-skinned form or a form with prominent ridges. The Lagenaria is also called Cucuzzi, New Guinea Butter Vine, or Italian Climbing Squash. Both Luffa and Lagenaria are rather good if eaten while still small (4-6 inches). The plants that produce this unusual vegetable are extremely vigorous and do best on a tellis. Luffas can also be used as sponges if allowed to mature. Soak them in running water until the skin decomposes, exposing a tough inner fiber which you can dry and bleach in the sun.

● **Climbing Spinach.** Not at all related to spinach, this tropical vine nevertheless tastes similar to it in a fresh salad with chopped pieces of boiled egg, vinegar, and a little oil. In addition to the standard green-stemmed variety *(Basella alba)*, there is also a red-stemmed variety *(Basella rubra)*. Both are vigorous vines an grow best on a trellis or fence.

● **Edible soybeans.** By themselves, these nutritious beans taste like little pieces of green cardboard, hardly worth growing. Try to remember how nutritious soybeans are and mix them with some sausage and perhaps a hot pepper or two for seasoning. Kanrich seems to be one of the more popular varieties, but the South is also adapted to culture of the late-season black soybean used as a dry bean in the Orient. Edible soybeans require about the same space that limas do. The green seed is hard to shell unless boiling water is first poured over the pods and allowed to cool.

● **Chayote (mirliton or vegetable pear).** This member of the squash family is adapted only to the lower South. It produces a vigorous vine which sometimes covers trees. Fruiting begins in the fall and may continue until January in mild years. Start plants by placing the entire fruit (it is usually allowed to sprout first) in the planting hole, with the large end pointing slightly down and the narrow end barely covered. If the roots are protected with a mulch in the winter the plant may be perennial. Mirlitons have little flavor and are usually stuffed with rich sauces.

● **Popcorn and Ornamental or Indian Corn.** These vegetables require about the same care as sweet corn. Interesting variations include Strawberry popcorn with short 1½ to 2-inch ears of mahogany-colored husks, and purple-husked Indian Corn with beautiful multicolored kernels and purple husks.

● **Unusual Eggplants.** Americans are familiar with the standard "Black Beauty" eggplant, but there are many others—in particular, the long, skinny oriental varieties and the small oriental varieties often used for pickling. These plants are smaller overall, but they are very productive.

● **Unusual Cucumbers.** Some interesting cucumbers to try in addition to the regular ones are:

Armenian Yard-Long Cucumber, a ribbed, light green, very mild and crunchy type best adapted to trellis culture; Burpless Cucumbers, long like the Armenian, but darker green, mild, and not quite as crunchy; Snake Cucumber, long like the first two, but twisted and curled; the Lemon Cucumber, round, about baseball-size, yellow, mild and burpless; and the Gherkin, the small spiney fruits of which make excellent pickles.

● **Horseradish.** Not as well adapted to the deep South as it is to more nothern areas, this root vegetable can still be grown with some success. Its problem seems to be in not getting a long enough dormant period.

● **Jicama.** This is a delightful vegetable. The part eaten is an underground tuber that looks like a rough-skinned grayish-brown turnip. It is peeled and sliced or grated for salads, but is just as good eaten off the vine. Its texture is similar to water chestnut, and the flavor seems to be a cross between English Pea and Apple. If desired, the plant can be grown as an ornamental, as it produces attractive flowers. For tuber production, however, it is necessary to keep the flowers picked off. Seed is usually not available, but the tubers offered in the grocery store can be planted several inches deep in a loose, well-draining soil.

● **Unusual Peppers.** This is one of the most diverse groups of vegetables. Between the hot and the bell pepper types, and all the degrees of pungency and different shapes within each type, the variations are almost infinite. One variety, Aconcagua, produces a mild pepper which often gets 18 inches long. Varieties like the Serrano Chile pepper aren't much more than an inch long and so hot they almost scald the tongue. If you are interested in peppers and decide to grow all of them you should be able to keep your garden replete with different peppers for some time.

● **Hot Weather Spinach Substitutes.** The first of these to gain some popularity is New Zealand Spinach. This vegetable thrives in hot weather. The tender growing tips of this plant are harvested for food. Climbing Spinach (Malabar) is a tropical vine discussed with standard vegetables because of the great increase in popularity it seems to be enjoying.

● **Unusual Squashes.** Specialty seed catalogs offer some interesting oriental varieties. Particularly notable are Kikuza White, Hyuga Early

Black, and hybrids by Sakata in Japan. These winter squash (for *storing* in winter, not growing) grow on long vines. They are generally of excellent quality, although their suitability to southern growing conditions remains to be tested.

● **Husk Tomato (Tomatillo).** This is another member of the *Solanacae* family, which includes tomatoes, peppers, and eggplants. The yellowish fruits are covered by a paper-like husk. The fruit is sweet but tart and is used in jams, jellies, and sauces. Plants require about the same care you would give tomatoes or peppers.

● **Air Potato** *(Dioscorea bulbifera).* This is a little-known vegetable. Inedible varieties are sometimes grown for ornament in the U.S., but edible varieties are commonly grown elsewhere. The air potato is a member of the true yam family and is an easily-grown potato substitute.

● **Unusual Vegetables.** Many vegetables come in unusual shapes and colors. For instance, there are purple podded beans (Royalty), white cucumbers (White Wonder), yellow cucumbers, green eggplants, golden eggplants, white eggplants (Albino and White Beauty), white zuchinni (White Courese), yellow zuchinni (Burpee Golden), round zuchinni (Round), orange and red striped tomatoes (Tigerella) and yellow watermelons (a new ice box variety is called Yellow Baby) just to name a few.

● **Jerusalem Artichoke.** When is an artichoke not an artichoke? The answer is simple—When it's a sunflower. The artichoke in question is the Jerusalem Artichoke, which, to further complicate matters, is not from Jerusalem. It's a perennial sunflower native to the northeastern United States.

This vegetable has only recently become popular in the home garden, although Indians grew it at the time the first settlers arrived in this country. Apparently, early explorers took it back to Europe calling it Girasole, which was mistakenly changed to Jerusalem. In any case, a more appropriate name currently being popularized is Sun Choke.

The plant looks like a sunflower should look, perhaps a bit smaller, and the flowers are not nearly as large as those of the common sunflower. The edible part is an oblong tuber that develops on the roots. Especially interesting is the fact that Sun Chokes contain the carbohydrate insulin, which is vital to persons with diabetes.

Hogs and other livestock like these tubers, but Sun Chokes are much too good for this use. Although the tubers can be cooked the same ways as potatoes, they're better raw in salads, where they lend a sweet, crunchy water-chestnut texture and flavor.

How do you grow them? One Houston gardener says he always plants his Sun Chokes in July. That way they mature tubers about frost time and you don't have to dig them in mid or late summer. They store well in the ground during cool weather (just dig a few as you need them), or they can be dug and stored in plastic bags in the refrigerator. If they're not stored in plastic they shrivel and deteriorate rapidly.

The Sun Choke is not particular about growing conditions, but it does like a well-draining soil, so plant it in raised beds. Whole tubers or pieces about the size of a golf ball can be used. These should be planted about 4 inches deep. They are usually planted 2 feet apart in the row, with rows 3½ feet apart. If you have trouble finding a source of tubers to plant, just use those available in the produce section of the grocery store. Although planting in July sounds like a good idea, tubers can also be planted in February or March.

Index